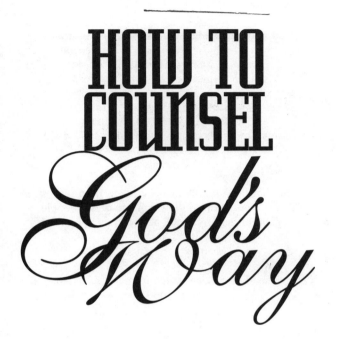

HOW TO COUNSEL
God's Way

by
Bob Hoekstra

ACKNOWLEDGEMENTS
OF GOD'S FAITHFULNESS

The Lord has demonstrated His faithfulness in numerous ways through many of His dear saints concerning the writing of this book. His primary blessing has come to me through my wife, Dini, who prayed for me and exhorted me faithfully. Next, the Lord encouraged me consistently through my father, Chaplain Ray, who developed a passionate heart for biblical counseling during his later years in life.

Early in the process of our counseling studies, Pastor Chuck Smith supported our broadcasting of these sometimes controversial messages over KWVE, the Calvary Chapel radio station for Southern California. This opened many doors of broad proclamation and extensive dialogue, which brought subsequent refinement of insight.

God also brought much encouragement through my dear friend and former ministry assistant, Pastor John Stewart. Long-time friend, Pastor Brian Brodersen, was also used of God in a significant manner through innumerable discussions and confirmations.

Invaluable contributions were made in the editing arena by Jan Manderson, Georgia Babb, and Shelly Bowles. These dear friends in Christ were exceedingly helpful both in literary perceptivity and spiritual discernment.

In addition to these few, so many others prayed or provided assistance that this book might be produced. Among them are Pastor Brad Lambert, Cheryl Brodersen, Lisa Stewart, Susan Moore, Bill Garrett, Ron and Evetta Bock, Joanne Bowles, and Gwen Weaver. Only the Lord knows their full number. For them all, we give praise and thanks to the Lord for His abundant faithfulness.

Dedication

This book is dedicated to the glory and the use of our Wonderful Counselor, the Lord Jesus Christ, with abundant thanks to Him for my wife, Dini, who for over 32 years has been the primary instrument of His counsel in my life.

Also, special gratitude is offered to the Lord for my father, Chaplain Ray Hoekstra of the International Prison Ministry, who encouraged me greatly in the writing of this book.
He had planned to publish this book until he went home to be with the Lord in November of 1997.

PREFACE

The burden and insight for this book developed during thirty years of serving the Lord as a Pastor. In teaching the scriptures, I witnessed the life-changing impact they had in people's daily walk. In studying the word of God, I began to see the rich message it contained concerning counseling. In counseling from the Bible, I observed the liberating and sanctifying power it unleashed in hungry or needy lives.

On the other hand, various sources of input brought a realization that many in the church world (including me) were not relying wholly upon God's word as they ministered. Books that earnestly contended for the faith sounded a warning about psychological theories being integrated with the word of God. Troubled Christians came to me for help describing their previous counseling in terms that neglected or contradicted the scriptures. Also, a growing number of phone-in Christian radio programs offered counsel that was heavily psychologized.

In the early 1990's, I was guided by the Lord into extensive study and teaching on the subject of biblical counseling. My intentions were to edify and protect the saints that God had entrusted to my care. Soon, I was accepting many invitations across the country and overseas to teach on this topic in a format of church seminars, leadership conferences, and Bible Colleges. This path soon became a full-time traveling ministry that has continued to increase to this day.

The approach of this book is that of a pastor, not of a researcher. My primary desire is to explore the word of God on these great matters of counseling, discipling, and personal ministry. This is not a research project detailing the various systems of psychological theory. Others have done excellent work in this area. The general references made to psychological theory in this book are given to provide spiritual contrasts and biblical warnings.

This book is written for everyone in the body of Christ, from the Staff Pastor to the caring homemaker to the responsible businessman. All of us are called to offer counsel regularly one to another. Each of us needs a word of counsel periodically. These studies are designed to assist us in learning to give godly counsel, as well as develop discernment in evaluating counsel that we or others might be receiving.

May the Lord Jesus use these studies to enlarge our vision of Him as our Wonderful Counselor.

Pastor Bob Hoekstra
California, 1999

TABLE *of* CONTENTS

SECTION FOUR:
Foundational Truths for Counseling

SECTION FIVE:
Major Threats to Counseling God's Way

Introduction:
Counseling God's Way

Introduction: A Crisis in Counseling

A tragic, growing crisis is facing the Lord's church concerning the ministry of counseling. An increasing number of churches and church leaders are forsaking God's way of counseling and turning to man's ways. They are relying more and more on psychological theories, and less and less on the truth of the word of God. They are looking to self for answers, instead of to the Lord. They are turning to the experts of the world, instead of to the family of God.

Many concerned Christians are developing the same apprehension for the church world today that the apostle Paul expressed in 2 Corinthians 11:3:

> *"But I fear, lest somehow, as the serpent deceived Eve by his craftiness, so your*

1

minds may be corrupted from the simplicity that is in Christ."

Two-Fold Approach

This book will address this problem in two ways. The primary approach will be to examine counseling and related matters from God's perspective in His word. To the surprise of many, scripture gives us a wealth of input in this area. The secondary approach will be to sound a strong warning from the scriptures concerning the attempts to integrate psychological theory with biblical truth in the counseling ministry. This is both a deadly and a predominating practice throughout the church world. In both approaches we desire to be . . .

> *"holding fast the faithful word as (we have) been taught, that (we) may be able, by sound doctrine, both to exhort and convict those who contradict"* (Titus 1:9).

"Umbrella Clichés"

Along the way, we will consider a number of "**Umbrella Clichés**" that are commonly used to explain or defend the use of psychology in counseling and personal ministry. A cliché is a popular saying that has such broad acceptance that many assume it settles the subject at hand as soon as the cliché is stated.

An umbrella provides shelter and protection. The **"Umbrella Clichés"** that will be discussed are providing defective, but often unchallenged, covering for humanistic, self-centered thinking in much of the church world. Clichés that we will focus on include:

- "People's problems are related to low self-esteem, so help comes in raising their self-esteem."
- "Well, at least people are getting some help out there."
- "We don't want to throw out the baby with the bath water."
- "All truth is God's truth."
- "Life's problems are too complex today to be using only the Bible and the Holy Spirit."
- "We must always be prepared to send the difficult counseling cases to the psychologically-trained experts, since they are the only ones who fully understand man and can thereby deal effectively with complex problems."
- "People's problems are rooted in the past, therefore we must extensively examine each person's past in order to discover solutions for the present."
- "People's lives are controlled by issues that are buried within their subconscious minds, therefore they must uncover these matters in order to find

real help."

- "You go to a body-doctor when your body is not functioning properly; so why won't you go to a mind-doctor when your mind is not functioning properly?"

All of these **"Umbrella Clichés"** present a persuasive argument to the natural mind. However, as we let the light of scripture shine upon them, we will see that they are all filled with holes. They do not stand up to the truth of God's word.

Prayer for Each Reader

The readers of this book will no doubt vary greatly in personal circumstances and individual roles in life. Some may be pastors or counselors or church leaders looking for direction or confirmation from the Lord in their ministries. Some may be parents or Christians who seek help in reaching out to hurting or troubled family members or friends. Some readers may be the ones in difficult situations or facing times of discouragement or despair. My prayer for all who read this book is three-fold:

- that each will **be personally counseled** by the Lord through any of His truth that appears within these pages. We all need a word of counsel from the

Lord periodically.

- that each will **be more fully equipped** to be used of Him in counseling and discipling and personal ministry with others. We are all called upon time and again to give a word of counsel to a friend or church member.
- that each will **be effectively warned** concerning the self-serving, man-centered thinking that is pouring into so-called Christian counseling through the wide-spread acceptance of psychological theory in the churches. We are all affected regularly by this subtle phenomenon.

SECTION ONE

A Biblical Perspective on Counseling

It is vital that we begin with a solid understanding of what counseling is and is not. If we begin with erroneous perspectives here, all of our subsequent conceptions about counseling will be adversely effected. Many misconceptions prevail concerning counseling. This causes even well-meaning people to offer ungodly counsel to others, or to fail to recognize godly counsel when they seek help themselves.

To properly give and receive counsel God's way, we need to have a **biblical perspective** on counseling. We often mistakenly think counseling is giving our best advice to others concerning felt needs or desired goals or necessary changes. Such a view of counseling typically deteriorates into offering human wisdom in an attempt to solve problems, reduce stress, remove perplexities, or develop a few more coping techniques.

Counseling God's way is on a completely different, and much higher, plane. We will see that it involves **the Lord as Counselor**, pointing out **His path of discipleship**, and unfolding **His process of sanctification**.

"And His name will be called Wonderful Counselor"
— Isaiah 9:6 (NASB)

Chapter 1
The Lord as Counselor

The irreplaceable starting point for counseling God's way is seeing **the Lord as counselor**. This truth is the absolute anchor in a biblical perspective on counseling. The Lord wants to be our counselor and guide through life. He has claimed that role for Himself.

> *"I will instruct you and teach you in the way which you should go; I will counsel you with My eye upon you"* (Psalm 32:8, NASB).

In the family of man, man counsels man. In the family of God, God counsels man. This difference is fundamental and vast.

For Those Who Respect God

This divine counseling takes place in the

lives of those who fear God. The counsel of God is revealed to those who respectfully trust and reverence Him.

> "Who is the man who fears the Lord? Him shall He teach in the way He chooses. The secret (intimate counsel) of the Lord is with those who fear Him"
> (Psalm 25:12, 14).

True counseling is God giving His authoritative and all-sufficient counsel for His ordained purposes in our lives. When this dynamic is occurring, we rely on the Lord to disclose the life He wants us to live. We can thereby develop the confident confession expressed in Psalm 73:24: "You will guide me with your counsel, and afterward receive me to glory."

The Example of David

King David of Israel was a man who looked to the Lord as his counselor. This reality is documented clearly and consistently throughout much of David's writings, including the most well-known expression of faith he ever made.

> "The Lord is my shepherd; I shall not want. He makes me to lie down in green pastures; He leads me beside the still waters. He restores my soul; He leads me in the paths of righteousness

for His name's sake" (Psalm 23:1-3).

As David trusted in the Lord to shepherd and guide his life, he allowed God to function as his counselor. Such trust brought David assurance that the Lord would lead him to nourishing pastures of divine truth, to refreshing waters of the Holy Spirit, to the supernatural renewing of the inner man, and to the right paths that would bring honor to God's name. We also have a great need today for these matters in our lives. We too can live in such expectation from the Lord, if we trust in Him to be our shepherd, our counselor.

Humanity in general, and many Christians in particular, vainly look to man to provide in human counsel what David found in the Lord as his counselor. We seek in man that which can be found in God alone. Again, David is an instructive example to us today, as seen in Psalm 62:5-8:

> *"My soul, wait silently for God alone, For my expectation* (my hope, NASB) *is from Him. He only is my rock and my salvation; He is my defense; I shall not be moved. In God is my salvation and my glory; The rock of my strength, And my refuge is in God. Trust in Him at all times, you people; Pour out your heart before Him; God is a refuge for us."*

Putting Our Expectations in the Lord

David put his hope in God alone. Since the Lord is our true and ultimate counselor, we want to set all of our expectations upon Him. God may, or may not, use human instruments as He counsels us. Either way, we would greatly benefit by investing a period of quiet waiting before the Lord.

The common tendency in seeking counsel is to spend all of our time talking about our troubles with whomever will listen to us. We will find much value in remembering that the Lord alone can be our rock of stability. He alone can be a fortress of protection to keep our lives from being shaken to pieces. He alone can provide sufficient rescue from the snares into which we fall. If anything glorious is to happen in our lives, it truly depends on Him. The strength we need to carry us through difficulties is also found in Him and Him alone.

Pouring Out Our Hearts to God

It is essential that we learn to depend upon the Lord more and more as our counselor. We express our dependence upon Him by pouring out our hearts before Him. The Lord already knows all that is within us. He simply wants us to come to Him habitually, laying out to Him all that is transpiring within us. Sometimes our hearts are filled with sadness, pain, bitterness, regret, fear, or confusion. Sometimes it includes thoughts or feelings that we imagine could never be shared with anyone. By taking them all to the Lord, we are looking to Him to function as our counselor.

The Wonderful Counselor

One of the names of the Lord, ascribed to the Son of God in Isaiah 9:6, makes it abundantly clear that He is to be our counselor: *"And His name will be called Wonderful Counselor"* (NASB). This prophetic word about Jesus Christ reveals one of the unique roles that the Son would fulfill when He came to earth as man, making the counsel of God even more personally clear and available. He would be the greatest counselor that could ever be sought by mankind. Among all the experts of humanity, there is no counselor who could ever measure up to Jesus Christ, the Wonderful Counselor.

Just how wonderful would the Lord be as a counselor? Colossians 2:3 answers that question in a profound way. Speaking of Jesus, this verse states, *"In whom are hidden all the treasures of wisdom and knowledge."* Counseling involves seeking the knowledge we need and the appropriate wisdom to use that knowledge properly. Such knowledge and wisdom are hidden in Christ. Truly, every heavenly treasure of wisdom and knowledge available to man is found in Jesus Christ.

This astounding truth is referring to the spiritual realm of life. In the Lord we will find all of the wisdom and knowledge needed for living life and growing in godliness as God desires. The Apostle Peter wrote of this in 2 Peter 1:3:

> *"As His divine power has given to us all things that pertain to life and godliness, through the knowledge of Him who called us by glory and virtue."*

Every measure of knowledge for under-standing problems, growing spiritually, or living godly is all there in Christ. Every aspect of wisdom to use that knowledge in facing the demands of life is all there in Jesus. Notice that we are not told that "many of them" or "most of them" or "all but a few of them" are found in Him. Rather, the radical fact is that **all** of these spiritual jewels are found in Christ.

Mining Heavenly Gold

We must realize that these divine riches are **hidden** in Him. However, they are not hidden to keep us from finding them; they are hidden so we must search in the only place where they are accessible. They are not lying around on pews, chairs, or couches for imme-diate possession by visiting church meetings, recovery groups, or therapy offices. These godly gems of truth are accessed by "digging into" a deepening relationship with the Lord Jesus Christ. This "digging" involves learning more about, and depending more upon, who Jesus is, all that He has accomplished, and all that He has provided.

It is so heartbreaking to see the people of God digging for counsel in the gravel pits of human thinking, expecting to find gold from heaven. Mining in the wrong place guarantees distraction and disappointment. The Lord Jesus Christ is the gold mine of heaven wherein are hidden all the treasures of wisdom and knowledge. In light of the kinds of problems and heartaches that people experience in these difficult days, more than ever we need a counselor who can counsel in wondrous ways. Thanks be to God, the Lord Jesus Christ is such a counselor.

Jesus and Needy Lives

Some of the words that Jesus Himself uttered confirm His ability to be our Wonderful Counselor.

> *"The Spirit of the Lord is upon Me, Because He has anointed Me to preach the gospel to the poor; He has sent Me to heal the brokenhearted, To proclaim liberty to the captives and recovery of sight to the blind, To set at liberty those who*

are oppressed; To proclaim the accept-
able year of the Lord"
　　(Luke 4:18-19).

The Lord Jesus Christ was sent forth from heaven to meet the deepest needs of those who are spiritually poor, broken inside, held captive, are without spiritual sight, or are circumstantially buried. Often, it is these very lives who seek earnestly to find counseling. Jesus is particularly desiring to counsel such needy souls today.

To the spiritually poor, who are ready to admit their carnal poverty, the Wonderful Counselor offers the good news that He has made provision for the forgiveness of sin. To the brokenhearted, those shattered by grief or despair, Jesus brings a true wholeness for the inner man. To the captives, those who are bound by destructive habits or addictions, He supplies freedom. To the blind, those who cannot see the truths of God's kingdom, He grants sight. To the oppressed, those who are buried in impossible situations, He can arrange release. To one and all alike, Jesus announces this present season of God's gracious acceptance of all who will come to Him humbly through His Son.

Jesus and Thirsty Souls

Other words of Jesus, spoken to the woman at the well, give further reason for people to look to Him as the counselor above all counselors.

> *"Whoever drinks of this water will thirst again, but whoever drinks of the water that I shall give him will never thirst. But the water that I shall give him will become in him a fountain of water springing up into everlasting life"*
> (John 4:13-14).

Here, Jesus is contrasting the earthly material resources that man can provide with the heavenly spiritual resources that He alone can furnish. Only the latter resources can satisfy and fulfill.

This truth has significant implications for all who are seeking or offering counsel. Everyone who turns to natural worldly counsel, anticipating relief from the dry cisterns of human theories, finds a counsel that cannot impart enduring benefits. On the other hand, those who look for supernatural heavenly counsel, expecting comfort from the flowing springs of divine wisdom, find an eternal counsel with timeless impact.

Furthermore, the spiritual water contained in the Lord's counsel not only quenches the yearnings of our souls, but it also becomes in us a well-spring of abundant life. Jesus elaborated on this glorious reality in John 7:37-38:

> *"If anyone thirsts, let him come to Me and*

drink. He who believes in Me, as the Scripture has said, out of his heart will flow rivers of living water."

Spiritual thirst, inner yearning for the realities of life as God designed it, drives many people to seek counseling. Jesus invites such parched souls to come to Him for the quenching of their thirst. Those who are thirsty must turn from all other options and substitutes and put their hope in what Christ can do for them.

Exercising such trust toward the Lord is likened to drinking of Him. When physically thirsty people come to a glass of water, they make its contents their own, trusting that it will meet their need. When spiritually thirsty people come to Jesus in faith, they are making what He offers their own. They are believing that He can satisfy this dry inner need as they count on Him.

Rivers of Living Water

At this point, an extraordinary phenomenon is taking place. The Lord not only deals with the thirst we have within, He also begins to fill our inner man with the life-giving presence of the Holy Spirit. This work of God inside us eventually overflows with the very same living water that satisfied our thirst. We thereby become channels to touch others with that same thirst-quenching water that filled us. Those who are counseled by the Wonderful

Counselor become His cup-bearers of living water in a dry and thirsty world.

Conclusion

The bedrock fundamental truth for counseling God's way is that **the Lord is the actual counselor.** Man is not the counselor. The psychologist and the psychiatrist are not the counselor. Not even the pastor is the counselor. Jesus is the counselor. He can, and will, use us in sharing His counsel, if we are committed to Him, to His paths, and to His means of counseling (which we will address later at some length). However, He alone is the Wonderful Counselor.

So the major implications of this fundamental truth that the Lord is the counselor are these: when we need counsel, we must look to the Lord Jesus Christ, and when others come to us for a word of counsel, we must point them to the Lord as well.

"Then He said to them all, 'If anyone desires to come after Me, let him deny himself, and take up his cross daily, and follow Me'." — Luke 9:23

Chapter 2
Counseling and Discipleship

To establish a biblical perspective on counseling, it is necessary to consider discipleship. True godly counseling must be related to the **path of discipleship**. The popular approach to counseling in the church world today is commonly disassociated from discipling. This serious mistake contributes to the growing problem of humanistic, self-centered counseling entrenching itself in churches and Christian organizations.

Many Christians and church leaders alike think of counseling as designed primarily to deal with stress and to remove perplexities. In counseling God's way, the Lord is not aiming merely at meeting needs or solving problems. Rather, He wants to use the needs and problems in lives to bring people onto the path of discipleship, if they are not yet following Him. If they are already believers in Jesus Christ, He wants to use their uncomfortable situations to move them on down the path of pursuing Him.

When hurting people request our help, many of us are quickly motivated to straighten things out. With this perspective, we are often tempted to think God's priority goal is to bring back a comfort zone. Thus, we attempt to leap in and say or do anything that might take the edge off the pain. This approach may actually get in the way of what the Lord wants to do.

This is not to infer that God is void of compassion. He loves to come to our aid. Nevertheless, in counseling God's way our Wonderful Counselor is not merely aiming at removing or meeting needs. Rather, He wants to use existing needs to bring spiritual progress in our lives.

There is something about being needy that can effectively humble the heart. The humbling process is highly desirable, because God gives grace to the humble. The Lord knows that in allowing needs to arise in our lives, He prepares our hearts for His work within us. So when folks come to us for counsel, this understanding of discipleship should impact what we share. The Lord wants to use the counsel that He gives us for them, to either bring them onto the path of discipleship, or to help move them on down that path.

In counseling and personal ministry, we want to aim as high as the Lord is aiming. Man often aims so much lower than the Lord does. We may attempt to change some circumstance through counseling. The Lord wants to use His counsel to touch our hearts and change our lives. The Lord intends discipleship to be viewed as an integral part of counseling.

The Overall Command to Make Disciples

The command that Jesus gave in Matthew 28:18-19 is His comprehensive overall instruction to His people until He returns:

> *"All authority has been given to Me in heaven and on earth. Go therefore and make disciples of all the nations."*

Everything we undertake in our own lives and in the life of the church is to be related to this one overriding purpose of making disciples. We who are the people of God must aim at making disciples wherever we go throughout the entire world. We are not commanded to build religious organizations. We are told to make disciples. We are not sent out to recruit all of the church members that we possibly can. We are sent to make disciples. We are not here to raise all of the funds that we can accumulate. We are here to make disciples. We are not directed to meet every human need or to remove every dilemma in life or to make people feel good about themselves. We are to make disciples.

In our thinking and functioning, we must never separate counseling from making disciples. Counseling is to be a part of building disciples. As we counsel God's way, we view each counseling situation as a discipling opportunity that has been stirred by some need or desire that has arisen in a person's life. So let us think together about what discipleship is and how this responsibility of making disciples is to affect our approach to counseling.

Following Jesus

Disciples are followers of Jesus Christ. Our Lord gave the basic call to discipleship in Matthew 4:19: *"Follow Me, and I will make you fishers of men."* Jesus, who is the Master, the Teacher, the Discipler, invites us to invest our lives in following after Him. Discipleship is a life-long, life-giving, life-changing, and life-developing relationship.

We pursue Jesus Christ, the Lord of glory, the Wonderful Counselor. Step by step along the way, He works on our lives and in our lives and through our lives. These consequences of living as a disciple flow from the hope-building promise that Jesus linked with His call to follow Him: *"I will make you fishers of men."*

These men who first heard Jesus' call had learned to catch fish with nets, for their own use. As they followed Him, they were taught how to catch men with the gospel, for the Lord's use. As we follow after Him, He is remaking us. Discipleship involves following Jesus, while desiring, expecting, and allowing Him to reshape our lives into whatever He wants us to be. Counseling is one strategic component of disciplemaking that the Lord will use to effect some of His desired changes in our lives.

The Terms of Discipleship

In Luke 9:23, Jesus stated the terms of discipleship. If anyone wants to answer Jesus' call to follow Him, here is what is involved.

> *"Then He said to them all, If anyone desires to come after Me, let him deny himself, and take up his cross daily, and follow Me."*

In a parallel passage, we are told who it was that Jesus was addressing.

> *"And He summoned the multitude with His disciples, and said to them"*
> (Mark 8:34, NASB).

These words were spoken to all who were in the crowd that day. These terms of discipleship were given to His followers and the mixed masses. Included in this wide spectrum of humanity were true followers, potential followers, curious onlookers, religious skeptics, angry scoffers, hungry seekers, and more. This throng was typical of the full range of humanity today. These terms are for everyone in every place and in every circumstance.

Denying Self

The first term of discipleship is that a person must deny himself. Those who want to follow Jesus are required to say no to the independent self-life. They are to confess and renounce the sins of **self**-righteousness, **self**-exaltation, **self**-will, and **self**-sufficiency. They are to reject the **self**-centered way of thinking and living. *"Let him deny himself."* These words are a call to repentance, a call to change our minds. In denying ourselves, we are agreeing with God that any life that we can produce will never be acceptable to Him. We must forsake the self-life and find a new life from Him.

Taking Up Our Cross

The second term of discipleship is that a person must take up his cross. When these words were spoken by Jesus, the cross was an instrument of execution. It was what a gallows or a gas chamber or an electric chair became in many contemporary cultures. On the cross, the most severe judgment was given to the worst offenders. Every individual who would be a disciple of Jesus Christ is to take up the instrument of his or her own execution. Luke 9:24 makes it clear that Jesus was speaking of death to the self-life:

> *"For whoever desires to save his life will lose it, but whoever loses his life for My sake will save it."*

The only cross that can fully deal with the self-life is the cross of Jesus Christ. On that cross Jesus died for all that we were or could ever hope to make of ourselves. He took the judgment that we deserved. He was alienated from the Father, taking upon Himself the divine wrath that we should have received for our sinful, selfish life.

Disciples must take up that cross, identifying with it. We put our trust and confidence in Christ and His work upon that cross. We carry His cross about as our logo, as it were. It defines our need. It holds forth our remedy and hope. In the cross of Christ we received the judgment that was truly ours. By faith, we died on that cross with Him. We found God's way to properly deal with the self-driven life.

This taking up of our cross is not a single,

isolated act. This is an on going attitude and perspective seen in the word "daily." Certainly, the scriptures declare that we are justified from sin (Romans 3:24) and given eternal life (John 1:12-13) the moment we believe on the Lord Jesus Christ. However, Luke 9:23 speaks not only of the act of repentance and faith that begins our walk with Christ, it also describes a confession and trust that should mark all of our walk with Him. Every day we are to say no to the self-life. Each day we are to take up the cross of Christ, admitting that apart from His work for us and in us, we would still deserve that same judgment. This day-by-day attitude deals with the basic continuing obstacle to following Jesus, and that is **self**.

Self-esteem

We live in a self-centered world. Most people grow up being taught and encouraged to "look out for number one," referring to self. Our society constantly bombards us with worldly and humanistic concepts that reinforce self. The high priority goals of the world in general seem to be **self**-fulfillment, **self**-determination, **self**-gratification, **self**-assertion, **self**-confidence, **self**-improvement, and **self**-affirmation.

When recognized experts on human behavior share their psychological theories on how to live life properly, they generally give an official sanction to the self-absorbed life. Abraham Maslow's hierarchy of needs pyramid, which culminates in self-actualization, would be a typical example. Thus, the common and popular counseling approaches tend to entrench the self-life, in spite of the growing numbers of devastated lives that are being produced by such self-indulgence.

The self-esteem movement has played a major role in establishing self-absorbed thinking and counseling in the church world. As psychological theory has been increasingly embraced and promoted by seminaries, denominations, and church leaders, the assumed need for self-esteem is now viewed by many as virtually a biblical absolute.

UMBRELLA CLICHÉ #1:
"People's problems are generally related to low self-esteem, so help comes through raising their self-esteem."

This umbrella cliché has done much to provide popular shelter for self-esteem counseling within the church world. Such thinking was not introduced into the church through biblical studies or through the teaching of the word of God. It came into the church from humanistic psychological theoreticians. It is a product of the principles and values of the world. Should this perspective on counseling be welcomed among the redeemed of the Lord?

Such self-indulgent ideas are moving in a different direction from the path to which the Lord has called us. If self-esteem counseling were only five or ten degrees off course, it would still be a serious problem. Every step taken down that path would lead one farther and farther off the proper path. However, the situation is far more devastating than that. Self-esteem counseling is one hundred eighty degrees off course. It points people in a direction opposite of where Jesus calls them. The Lord calls us to say "no" to our self-life and to lose it for His sake. The self-esteem call urges us to affirm ourselves and learn to hold ourselves in higher and higher regard.

We should not be amazed that the world is looking to self for hope and fulfillment. However, we should be shocked and burdened that the church has become deeply committed to this same self-focused perspective in counseling. Our Lord and Master has commanded us to deny ourselves. Contrary to this, many church leaders insist that attention must be given to helping people strengthen their self-life.

At this point in Jesus' call to discipleship, some may wonder what is left. Denying self and taking up the cross sounds like the end of everything. Actually, this is always the beginning of all that God yet desires to do in our lives.

Again, Following Jesus

In the last three words of Luke 9:23, we return to the heart of discipleship: *"and follow Me."* This invitation tells us how to find all that we will ever need for time and eternity. Also, it indicates how God accomplishes His will in, and through, us. God works His good pleasure in our lives as we follow after His Son, the risen Lord and Savior Jesus Christ, the Wonderful Counselor, in whom are hidden all the treasures of wisdom and knowledge.

When man asks us to follow self, there is no possibility of finding what only God can provide. However, when Jesus calls us to follow Him, this changes everything. The difference has to do with the nature of the Christian life and the reality of who Jesus is.

The Christian life is a resurrection life. Jesus is the resurrected Lord. The resurrected life we need can only be found in a resurrected Lord. Furthermore, such a life can only be developed by following a resurrected Lord. The counsel that we need, and should be offering to others, must center around such fundamental discipleship truths.

Many people stagger at this fact that all we need can be found in merely following Jesus. This is basically related to their underestimating of who Jesus is and all that He has done and all that He now provides. In Him we can find all that God has for us to live full and complete lives.

"For in Him dwells all the fullness of the Godhead bodily; and you are complete in Him" (Colossians 2:9-10).

The fullness of what God offers to man is found in Jesus. In His fullness, we find our completeness. Forgiveness is found in following Jesus. Hope is found in following Him. Knowledge and wisdom are found in following Him. Strength and peace are found in following Him. A home in heaven is our destiny as we pursue Him. A new life filled with fruitfulness on earth is our portion as we follow the Lord Jesus Christ. You name it. If we need it, and if God has ordained it for us, it is found in following Jesus. We will give much more attention to these matters in a later section on "Foundational Truths for Counseling God's Way."

A Reminder of the Self Problem

So, discipleship is following the Lord Jesus Christ. Why are many not following Him, both initially and continually? Probably because they do not want to say no to self and embrace the cross for more death to self. They are still building their own lives. They think they can do it by themselves and for themselves. The cross does not yet look like their only option. In so many counseling situations, this is a critical issue to examine with those who seek our help.

Counseling Illustration

Some time ago, I sat with a couple that had endured a difficult marriage for many years. They took turns blasting each other, attempting to convince me that their mate was the basic problem in their home. The husband tore into the wife, listing her failures and shortcomings. The thrust of his diatribe implied that I was to help him remake her into the image that he desired in a wife.

Just when I was feeling great compassion for his wife (and a strong urge to choke him?!?), she made it clear that she was not looking for my protection. She attacked him verbally, making him sound like the worst husband in the history of marriage. Frequently, she looked at me, indicating that I should do something to help her change him into the man she wanted him to be.

While they were lashing out at each other, I was doing three of the eight or so things that I customarily give attention to in a counseling setting. (We will give extended consideration to these matters later in Chapter Eleven.) I was (1.) listening, (2.) praying, and (3.) noting any scripture that the Lord would bring to mind for this heartbreaking situation. One verse came persistently to my mind.

I asked them if we could let the Lord in on the conversation, allowing Him to say something to us through His word that might begin to rectify their plight. They indicated that they realized their need to hear from the Lord. I opened the word and read Luke 9:23:

"Then He said to them all, 'If anyone desires to come after Me, let him deny himself, and take up his cross daily, and follow Me'."

Turning to the husband, I asked him to go back over all of his accusations against his wife in light of this verse. I thought he was going to fall off his chair. He began to stammer, muttering disjointed words that implied God had closed his mouth with a sense of conviction and accountability. What could this husband say? All of his previous remarks had been about self-interest and self-righteousness and self-will. One precise word from the Lord cut through all of the carnal complaining and revealed the true issue. He, as well as his wife, were living for self.

Very often the word of counsel that is needed for couples enduring a consistently troubled marriage is a reminder of the most basic term of discipleship, saying no to self. A great many marriage problems are rooted in too much self and too little discipleship. Real followers of the Lord Jesus Christ learn more and more to let the Lord deal with the relational challenges that occur in the household. Those who are not following the Lord typically take all of these difficult family developments into their own hands. They use their own wisdom, for their own purposes. They rely on their individual willpower, for their personal benefit and glory. Such self-centered approaches are a violation of the path of discipleship.

The growing list of grievances that disenchanted mates develop through years of marital battle is characteristically tied into selfish thinking and behaving by one or both marriage partners. When either mate is willing to deny self, take up the cross daily, and follow Jesus as a genuine disciple, there is room for God to work in that home. When both partners are truly willing to have self dealt with by the Lord, wondrous transformation can be consistently provided by Him. This is one of a multitude of situations that illustrate why discipleship is a fundamental part of counseling God's way.

Conclusion

In order to establish a biblical perspective on counseling, we first considered the fact that everything stands on this truth: **the Lord is the Counselor**. Now, a second truth has been added: the Lord wants to counsel people in **the path of discipleship**. By His counsel, He desires to either bring them onto that path or advance them along it.

The major implication of this second truth is that discipleship must flavor all of the counsel that we give or receive. We are not to seek or offer counsel that merely relieves discomfort and leaves the self-life untouched by the Lord.

In the next chapter, we will consider one more biblical truth involved in developing a biblical perspective on counseling. This truth involves counseling and **sanctification**.

"For this is the will of God, your sanctification."
— 1 Thessalonians 4:3

Chapter 3
Counseling and Sanctification

In our pursuit of a biblical perspective on counseling, we have considered **the Lord as Counselor** and **the path of discipleship**. The third aspect we will look at is **the process of sanctification**. God wants to use His counsel to sanctify us as we walk through the battles of life. Sanctification means being set apart for God's purposes, His use, and His glory. Whenever Christian counseling is patterned after, or integrated with, the psychological theories of man, the process of sanctification is neglected or diminished.

Past Sanctification

Sanctification can be viewed from the

three vantage points of past, present, and future. The sanctification that has already been accomplished in the past for the people of God is spoken of in 1 Corinthians 1:2:

> *"To the church of God which is at Corinth, to those who have been sancti-fied in Christ Jesus, saints by calling"* (NASB).

When we came to Christ, God set us apart from the world for His purposes, use, and glory. In this sense, we have already been sanctified in the past. Sometimes, in sharing the counsel of the Lord with another believer, we need to share this significant truth. This reminds us of one of the works of God on our behalf. It also reminds us of why we are here on this earth now.

Future Sanctification

The sanctification that is yet future is alluded to in Philippians 3:20-21:

> *"For our citizenship is in heaven, from which we also eagerly wait for the Savior, the Lord Jesus Christ, who will transform our lowly body that it may be conformed to His glorious body, according to the working by which He is able even to sub-due all things to Himself."*

Some day in the future, when our Lord

returns for His people, we will be fully set apart for His purposes, use, and glory. We will be glorified. Sin, carnality, and selfishness will be completely removed. Ultimately, we will dwell in the new heaven and new earth wherein only righteousness dwells. We will be fully sanctified. At times, in counseling situations, future sanctification is an important truth upon which to expound. Such truth builds hope, comfort, and assurance.

Present Sanctification

The present sanctification process is of special interest to us. It is the one that most commonly needs attention in our ministry of counseling one another. Present sanctification is all about growing in godliness now. Day by day our lives are made increasingly usable in the hands of the Lord, as we are set apart more and more for His purposes and His glory.

1 Thessalonians 4:3-4 speaks of this present process of sanctification:

> *"For this is the will of God, your sanctification: that you should abstain from sexual immorality; that each of you should know how to possess his own vessel in sanctification and honor, not in passion of lust, like the Gentiles who do not know God."*

Sexual Purity

The general issue here is sanctification. The particular area of concern is sexual purity. Past sanctification, which is accomplished by our being in Christ Jesus, does not automatically provide sexual purity every day thereafter. Future sanctification, which is ours in heaven, will never have to deal with sexual impurity, since only righteousness will prevail there. Clearly, our present sanctification is the issue here.

This sexual purity aspect of sanctification is becoming increasingly critical in biblical counseling. As our culture goes deeper and deeper into sensualism and worships at the idol of sexual indulgence, more and more counseling needs to relate to sexual purity.

The world walks in lustful passions. They do not know how to keep their bodies under honorable control. Temptation abounds, and sexual indulgence is commonplace. We who know God are to walk in purity.

Many of God's children today would profit from a word of counsel concerning such purity. Too many believers (especially those recently saved) are in sexual bondage at the worst, or in compromise at the least. They are stumbling in habits, thoughts, words, or attitudes. God desires to use His counsel to bring sanctification into these areas.

Comprehensive Sanctification

Note, however, that sexual impurity is only one specific example of the general will of God, which is our comprehensive sanctification. Even for the many children of God who do not struggle with sexual immorality, His desire to sanctify us must be a consistent component of the counsel that we offer or seek. The Lord wants to set our lives apart more and more in every way for His glory and purposes and use. 2 Timothy 2:21 speaks of this truth:

> *"Therefore if anyone cleanses himself from the latter, he will be a vessel for honor, sanctified and useful for the Master, prepared for every good work."*

This verse refers to a life being cleansed from things displeasing to the Lord, so that a person might be increasingly set apart for greater use by Him.

Not Mere Coping Techniques

How does this issue of progressive sanctification contribute to our understanding of counseling? It informs us that the counsel we give must be a part of, and in accord with, the sanctification process. So many people who go for counseling are merely seeking after another coping technique. Their goal is to either escape or endure their struggles.

The Lord intends much greater benefits in the counsel He has for us. He wants to sanctify our lives continually, not just teach us how to survive each day. He wants to change our lives day by day, making us more and more like His Son, the Lord Jesus Christ. If we are going to counsel God's way, our counsel must be aimed at sanctification.

Psychological Obstruction

Psychological counseling cannot contribute to sanctification. Sanctification is a work of God, by His Spirit, using His truth. Psychological theory is a human system of wisdom aiming, in part, at increasing a person's ability to change his own life through his own human resources. Consequently, psychological theory cannot contribute to the sanctification process. In fact, it gets in the way, obstructing what God desires to do. This crucial contrast between philosophical humanism and biblical truth will be addressed throughout this book.

> **UMBRELLA CLICHÉ #2:**
> **"Well, at least people are getting some help out there."**

This umbrella cliché is sometimes interposed at this point. It is applied to those seeking assistance in the so-called Christian psychological counseling clinics. If someone is getting valid biblical help from such clinics, wonderful. However, an important issue to raise is whether or not they are getting God's help God's way. To the extent that a counseling service emphasizes the Lord and His word, some of His answers for needy lives may actually be coming forth from that organization. On the other hand, if the counseling offered involves the integration of psychological theories, the damaging influence of humanistic thinking cannot be prevented, even by periodic references to Bible passages.

No Sweeping Condemnation

These statements are not expressed to condemn every counselor who ever studied psychology or has a degree in psychology. Some who are trained in psychology have been able to lay aside such human wisdom and have learned to rely wholly upon the word of God. Additionally, this line of reasoning does not mean that everyone who ever went to counseling in a Christian psychological clinic is being condemned. Furthermore, this line of thought does not infer that no one ever got any real help from God in counseling centers.

Some psychologically inclined counselors who do know the Lord might have considerable respect for God's word and for the power of prayer. They might have godly compassion for people. They might even have the spiritual gift of counseling (which will be dealt with later). Consequently, many spiritual realities are available for God to use in reaching lives. However, operating in some of these valid aspects of godly counsel does not justify attempts to borrow from man's psychological ways of counseling. God wants to offer His help His way.

Summary of A Biblical Perspective on Counseling

The Lord wants to give us an increasingly biblical perspective on counseling. Viewing counseling more and more the way that God does can impact our counseling ministry more than any other issue.

This perspective includes three fundamental issues. First, **the Lord is the counselor**, not man and his theories. So, we must look to the Lord when we seek counsel, and we must point to the Lord when we give counsel.

Second, **the path of discipleship** must permeate our approach to counseling. Our counsel must deal with the independent self-life, so that people can follow after Jesus Christ more fully. To put it another way, our counseling must not just aim at relief, but at discipleship.

Third, **the process of sanctification** should

significantly impact our understanding of counseling. Sanctification is the process of growing in godliness, in Christ's likeness. As we counsel, we are not aiming at helping people cope or helping them indulge their own desires. We want to assist them in fulfilling the Lord's desire that they be more fit for His use, set apart for His glory.

When the Lord uses us as an instrument to share His counsel, He will at times want us to help the person who is seeking counsel to gain a more biblical understanding of counseling. Otherwise, they may tend to discount or reject what we are sharing from God's word, mistakenly thinking that it is not "sufficiently psychological" to meet contemporary needs.

Let us ask the Lord to work these truths deeply into our own lives and the lives of His people, making us those who increasingly counsel His way.

Now, in the next section, we are going to look at the four basic means that God uses in bringing His counsel to us.

SECTION TWO

God's Means in Counseling

We have clearly seen that the Lord is to be our counselor, not man. Next, we will consider how He gets His counsel to us. He uses: **His word**, **the Holy Spirit**, **prayer**, and **church-life**. All four are to be in operation in order for us to fully experience counseling God's way.

Again, we are looking into another vital issue pertaining to counseling. When we fail to understand the means that God has ordained for counseling, we can easily be drawn aside into that which is popular and attractive, but counter-productive, or at best, less than God intends. This will explain why many people who are seeking help often resort to placing their hope in self-help books, human theories, recovery programs, and Christian psychological clinics. They are unaware of the means that God has established for making His divine counseling resources accessible to man.

> "Your testimonies also are
> my delight and my counselors."
> — Psalm 119:24

Chapter 4
God's Word in Counseling

In Psalm 119:24, we begin to see the place of **the word of God** in counseling as He designed it: *"Your testimonies also are my delight and my counselors."* The word of the Lord is the basic means He uses to get His counsel into lives. The Lord is the counselor. It makes perfect sense biblically that He would counsel us through His own word. God wants us to delight in His word. Then, as we give eager attention to it, He imparts His counsel to us.

Another insightful passage to consider is Psalm 19:7-11. If we meditate on these truths, we will see many reasons why we must be committed to the scriptures alone in our coun-

seling. Also, our confidence in God's word
will be greatly strengthened.

> *"The law of the LORD is perfect, convert-
> ing the soul; The testimony of the LORD is
> sure, making wise the simple; The statutes
> of the LORD are right, rejoicing the heart;
> The commandment of the LORD is pure,
> enlightening the eyes; The fear of the
> LORD is clean, enduring forever; The
> judgments of the LORD are true and right-
> eous altogether. More to be desired are
> they than gold, Yea, than much fine gold;
> Sweeter also than honey and the honey-
> comb. Moreover by them Your servant is
> warned, And in keeping them there is
> great reward."*

Able to Restore Lives

In this series of declarations, the character
and ability of God's word are linked together.
The first declaration in verse eight reveals the
perfection that characterizes the scriptures.
They are *"perfect,"* complete and flawless.
No necessary thing is missing from them. No
mistakes are included in them. Consequently,
the word of God is able to convert the soul.
It can restore our lives, renewing, reviving,
and rebuilding them. The word of the Lord is
able to put lives back together the way God
intended them to be. So many people are
searching for a way to have their lives

restored. God's perfect word has that unique capability.

Able to Give Wisdom

In addition to being perfect, the word of God is *"sure."* It has a divine certainty and infallibility about it. This is why it is able to make the simple wise. Note, however, who qualifies to receive wisdom from God's word. Humble, modest, unpretentious people are the ones who gain the wisdom of God from the scriptures. Those who are satisfied with their own wisdom cannot find true wisdom, even if they give periodic attention to the Bible. God's wisdom is given through His word to those who admit that they need it. Actually, great numbers of those who are seeking counseling are in desperate need of this wisdom that God alone can provide.

Able to Impart Inner Joy

In verse eight, God's word is further described as being *"right."* It is the absolutely correct way to think and to live. So, it rejoices the heart. It produces a joy deep down inside by revealing to us the only valid way to face every aspect of life here on earth, while also preparing us for heaven with the Lord. Being committed to the word and walking in it rejoices the heart.

Many people have little or no joy in their

hearts. Sometimes, such a joyless condition exists because they have no interest in or knowledge of the right way. They are trying to find what they think will work for them, instead of seeking after what God has for them. There is great joy in the right ways of the Lord. If our answers for life are found in God's word, we can find this joy. We can direct others to this joy, if we let our counsel come from the scriptures alone.

Able to Bring Enlightenment

Purity is another quality of the word of God, as described in verse eight. There are no impurities, no admixtures, no additives in the Bible. It is free from anything that would diminish or damage life as God intended it to be lived. As we minister the scriptures to those in need, the pure word of the Lord is offering to them or nurturing in them untainted spiritual life. Thereby, the light of God's pure word can shine out from inside, enlightening their eyes.

Able to Provide Enduring Impact

Verse nine implies that the scriptures produce fear or godly respect toward the Lord. This fear of the Lord is clean. There is no corrupting influence in it. Nothing is there to destroy or dissipate lives. This work of the word of God is clean, and it endures forever.

This enduring quality of God's word brings to mind 1 Peter 1:24-25:

"All flesh is as grass, and all the glory of man as the flower of the grass. The grass withers, and its flower falls away, but the word of the Lord endures forever."

The "glorious theories" that man produces are very similar to grass, which may seem impressive for a moment, but soon fades away. What we give people from God's word can have an eternal impact on their lives.

Able to Disclose Reality

All of God's pronouncements in His word are true: *"The judgments of the LORD are true."* They are accurate. They depict absolute reality. Christians inadvertently overlook this fact at times, even when we are departing from our church services. Someone will comment on it being time to "return to the real world." Seldom do we stop to consider that this is stating it backwards. The world that we are preparing to return to is a place of futility and fantasy and vain imaginations. It is filled with proud and lofty speculations lifted up against the ways of God. That supposed "real world" will someday be gone forever.

Actually, those who have gathered in the name of Jesus Christ are the ones living in the real world: the kingdom of God. It is a kingdom founded upon truth and substance, not lies and empty wishes. This authentic "real world" is revealed in the scriptures. The word of God is true and righteous altogether, correct in every aspect.

Able to Enrich and Satisfy

In verse 10, the word of the Lord is shown to be more desirable than great riches: *"More to be desired are they than gold, Yea, than much fine gold."* Many a person seeking counseling needs to hear this truth. Too many people are motivated merely by the pursuit of earthly treasures. Not only are those the wrong treasures to chase after, but they are also a major cause of the spiritual poverty that plagues multitudes of lives.

Also, verse 10 adds that the word of the Lord is designed to be more satisfying to the spirit than even honey is to the taste: *"Sweeter also than honey and the honeycomb."* The emptiness that torments the masses of humanity can be replaced by the deep spiritual satisfaction that the Lord brings through His word.

Able to Warn and Reward

Verse 11 states that God's word warns everyone who follows Him: *"Moreover by them Your servant is warned."* Every servant of God is given warning from the scriptures. All of us need to receive warnings from the

Lord. The dangers of the world, the flesh, and the devil pose a constant threat.

In addition to giving warning to all who will listen, God's word brings blessing to all who will obey it: *"In keeping them there is great reward."* As important as it is to hear the word of the Lord, there is another vital factor involved: *"But be doers of the word, and not hearers only"* (James 1:22). The heart's desire must be to respond to what God has said. Then, as we respond in humility and faith and obedience, God's word imparts His wonderful realities into our lives.

Contrasted with Psychological Theory

At this point, a reflective comparison between the word of God and psychological theory would be appropriate and helpful. Our study on counseling God's way is primarily a biblical exposition of what the Lord has commanded and provided for setting people free and making them whole. This book is not intended to be a detailed examination of psychological theory. Nevertheless, frequent observations and warnings regarding such theories will be necessary since these psychological perspectives are replacing biblical truth in so many churches today.

The verses that we have considered in Psalm 19 listed some of the wonderful things that God's word can do. It restores lives,

gives wisdom, imparts joy, brings enlightenment, provides enduring impact, and discloses
reality. It also enriches, satisfies, warns, and
rewards those who give heed to it. These
capabilities are all consequences of the character of the word, which was revealed as perfect, sure, right, pure, clean, and true.

For a moment, let's contrast the character
of the word with that of psychological theory.
These theories represent man's best opinions
about humankind's mental and emotional
components, observable behavior, change and
development, and related issues of person-
hood. These theories often include statements
about what is normal or abnormal, what is
healthy or unhealthy, and what is desirable or
undesirable. Usually, these opinions supply
definitions of, and proposed solutions for,
man's problems, needs, and challenges in life.

Remember the terms that characterize the
word of God: perfect, sure, right, pure, clean,
and true. The psychological theories of man
could justifiably be characterized (at least, in
part) as quite the opposite: imperfect, unsure,
incorrect, impure, unclean, and untrue. Such
a strong statement is not being too harsh on
man, since man's best guesses could never
measure up to God's absolutely reliable
knowledge given to us through His word.
This is why God wants us to rely wholly on
His word in counseling. Correspondingly, this
is why many pastors, church counselors, and

personal disciplers are setting aside man's psychological theories and are looking exclusively to the scriptures in their ministries.

UMBRELLA CLICHÉ #3:
"We don't want to throw out the baby with the bath water."

The umbrella cliché that is usually mentioned at this juncture is perhaps the one most frequently used. It often arises like this. First, a measure of acceptance is voiced concerning the validity and importance of using the Bible in counseling. Next, an appeal is usually made pertaining to possible contributions that psychological theory can make. Then, the umbrella cliché is announced: "**We don't want to throw out the baby with the bath water.**"

The baby in that cliché represents some assumed and necessary good within the theories of man. The bath water symbolizes something unhealthy or unhelpful within those theories. This cliché seems to offer a way for Christians to acknowledge that there are harmful elements in psychological speculations, while at the same time inferring that we will lose important counseling resources if we set all of this human wisdom aside.

Weakness of the Cliché

This cliché on the "baby-and-the-bathwater" reflects popular thinking concerning the role of psychology in so-called Christian counseling. Perhaps we can commend the desire to lose nothing that would be of true spiritual value in ministering to people. However, as with every other umbrella cliché that we will consider, this one does not stand up in the light of God's word.

The fallacy in this platitude can be uncovered in this manner. For the sake of argument, let us grant that there may be a baby sitting in the dirty bath water of psychological theory. What if we throw out the whole system of psychological speculations in our approach to the ministry of counseling. Have we lost the baby? Not at all, because even if we "tossed out the baby with the bath water," that baby can still be found in the word of God.

The Lord has revealed to us in His word the knowledge of Himself that gives us *"all things that pertain to life and godliness"* (2 Peter 1:3). Consequently, if there is anything in man's theorizing that appears clean and true, or seems helpful and needful, it will already be contained in the word. Furthermore, the scriptures have no unclean water that we have to filter out and set aside, since God's word is perfect, sure, right, pure, clean, and true.

The Liberating Truth of God's Word

In John 8:31-32, we can see another great

reason why we should rely wholly upon the word of God in our counseling, discipling, and personal ministry:

> *"Then Jesus said to those Jews who believed Him, 'If you abide in My word, you are My disciples indeed. And you shall know the truth, and the truth shall make you free'."*

Those who are truly functioning as genuine disciples of Jesus Christ are those who live in the word of God. Abiding in the word is one essential aspect of living as a disciple. Some people say they are disciples of the Lord Jesus Christ, yet the Bible has almost no place in their lives. That is not real discipleship. Those who follow Jesus live in His word. They hang on everything He has to say through His word. They read the word and are eager to hear it taught. They have personal times of Bible study and take part in group studies whenever possible. They are looking to Jesus and listening intently to Him. They really are His disciples.

Real disciples get into God's word habitually to find light, hope, strength, guidance, priorities and more. Then, by living in His word, they get to know the truth of His word. They are thereby increasingly set free by that truth. There is liberating power in the truth of the word of God.

Certainly, liberating power is what so many people desperately need. In the world, everyone is in bondage, even though they may not know it. In the church, too many are in bondage, even though they often deny it. Thus, a significant portion of counseling ministry involves people who need to be set free from all kinds of bondage.

This bondage is referred to by many terms. Some might call it bad habits. Others might call it addictions. Whatever the terminology, they are things from which we need to be set free. Sometimes, it is confused thinking. Sometimes, it is erroneous thinking. It may be compromised values or improper relationships. There are so many things from which God desires to liberate us.

Pictured by Lazarus

Lazarus was raised from the dead by the spoken word of the Lord: *"Lazarus, come forth!"* (John 11:43). Then, Jesus instructed those who were already among the living to assist Lazarus: *"Free him from the burial wrappings and let him go"* (verse 44, Amplified). Lazarus was now alive, but he was greatly hampered by the grave clothes that were wrapped around him.

Every Christian comes out of the spiritual grave of sin and death and blindness with numerous layers of dead wrappings. These wrappings are comprised of wrong thoughts, attitudes, and activities developed in the days before Jesus brought us new birth. One of our profound ministries to one another is to share the liberating truth of God's word, so that we can be set free from the grave clothes that bind our thinking, our relating, and our behaving. Knowing reality from God's perspective is finding ultimate reality. This brings divine liberation from the delusions we had known before following Christ.

The Sanctifying Truth of God's Word

In John 17:17, we see why God's intention is to use His word to bring us the counsel that we need. In Jesus' magnificent prayer to the Father just before the cross, He prayed on behalf of His followers: *"Sanctify them by Your truth; Your word is truth."*

We saw earlier that it is the will of God that our lives become increasingly sanctified. Remember, sanctification includes lives being set apart for the glory and purposes and use of the Lord. God sanctifies lives by the truth of His word. If we want to see people living for God's glory, rather than their own, then we must be sharing the truth of His word with them. If we hope to see people walking in line with God's purposes, then we will point them to the truth of the scriptures. If we desire to see people used of God, then the word of God will be our resource when we minister to them. It is by the truth of the word of God that lives are sanctified. Psychological theory cannot cause or contribute to the sanctification process, since its focus on self encourages people either to live for self or draw upon the inadequate and unacceptable resources of self.

UMBRELLA CLICHÉ #4:
"All truth is God's truth."

This may be the most significant umbrella cliché of them all. It customarily surfaces whenever the truth of God's word is declared to be essential to counseling God's way. It is the banner cry of those who are committed to integrating psychological theory with the truth of God's word. This cliché was endorsed by some of the faculty at the biblically-oriented seminary that I graduated from in 1973. Today, that seminary, as well as virtually every other evangelical seminary in the country, has adopted the thinking contained in this cliché as a part of their educational approach.

Some Dire Consequences

Such a perspective has monumental implications. One ramification is that psychological experts are included in school faculties in order to train pastors and Christian leaders how to counsel and minister to their congregations. Another related consequence of embracing this cliché is that seminaries and

Bible colleges develop full-blown departments of "Christian psychology" (which term has been denounced by some concerned observers as a misleading oxymoron). These departments are not apologetic in nature as they should be, that is, designed to examine psychology and to warn God's people of its errors. Rather, they are promotional and instructive in nature, being designed to inculcate psychological speculation into the overall approach to ministry.

The Reasoning behind This Cliché

The reasoning behind the "all-truth-is-God's-truth" cliché usually goes something like this. Since the Creator of all things is true, then any truth found anywhere must somehow find its source in Him. So when we find information or pronouncements in the fields of human learning that appear to be true, we can integrate them into biblical ministry, because "all-truth-is-God's-truth." Under this umbrella cliché are hidden vast measures of psychological counseling within the church world.

Many church leaders are regularly exposed to psychological counseling theories through their education or reading or interaction with one another. Whatever seems to be valid or sounds somewhat accurate or looks like it is "working" is often incorporated right into their approach to ministry in counseling and teaching. After all, these are the "social sciences" with which we are dealing, so we can trust in the conclusions that they bring to us.

One Fallacy of This Cliché

One erroneous aspect of this cliché has to do with the very nature of the field from which psychological input comes to us. Only a portion of these so-called social sciences has to do with real science, that is, an approach whereby conclusions or conjectures could be verified and reproduced in controlled experiments. Some psychological studies are essentially scientific, such as, conclusions derived from experimenting with four-year-old children to see what that age group can or cannot understand. The results of such studies only tend to demonstrate aspects of creation as God designed it. Such information is neither forbidden nor necessary for developing a life of godliness.

However, the social sciences could more accurately be named the **"behavioral philosophies,"** since their precepts are more like a philosophy of life than a true science. This is especially applicable to psychological theory. Psychology in application and emphasis appears to be much more engrossed with matters like "How to be Freed from Guilt Feelings" than with "How to Teach Appropriate Concepts to Differing Age Groups of Children."

The Smorgasbord of Integrated Truth

One of the tragedies of the "all-truth-is-God's-truth" thinking is that God's revealed truth and man's discovered truth are both brought to inappropriate levels. The incomparable and infallible truth of God's word is not prized as highly as it always should be. Conversely, man's mundane and questionable truth is treasured more highly than it ever should be. The result is that both categories of truth are offered upon the common level of one great smorgasbord of integrated truth.

From this tantalizing table, Christian counselors and church leaders select contemporary combinations of Philippians and Freud, Matthew and Maslow, Romans and Rogers. Whenever an objection is voiced to this unhealthy blending of incompatible foods, the servers reassuringly point to the banner above the table, which reads, "**ALL TRUTH IS GOD'S TRUTH.**"

The Promotion of Experiential Truth

Another application of this cliché promotes man's "subjective experiential truth" as having a value similar to God's objective scriptural truth. This approach reduces special revelation (the word of God) to the same level as general revelation (the creation) and natural theology (reflective reasoning). In this outlook, God has a variety of equal means through which He brings ultimate truth to humanity. Consequently, such matters as social history, personal observation, and human conscience are placed on a virtual equal footing with the scriptures. Again, when objections are raised against this mode of thinking, the reassuring response is to reiterate that "all-truth-is-God's-truth."

God's Exaltation of His Word

Certainly, the word of God indicates that He uses creation (Psalm 19:1-6) and history (1 Corinthians 10:1-11) and reasoning (Isaiah 1:18-20) and the conscience (Romans 2:14-15) as He works among mankind. However, these instruments of God's work are **all subject to the word of God**. They are not on the same level as His word. God's written word must give to us the proper understanding of these elements that lie outside of the scriptures, if such matters are to help us in comprehending or applying His ultimate truths.

God's ultimate truths are learned as we diligently get into the scriptures, which are called "the word of truth."

> *"Be diligent to present yourself approved to God, a worker who does not need to be ashamed, rightly dividing the word of truth"* (2 Timothy 2:15).

As we allow the Lord to sort out the many

aspects of the truth of His word, we will gain His approval and not be ashamed of our use of these other instruments of His working among us.

Furthermore, God has exalted His word of truth even higher than His name, which is far above all else that exists.

> *"I will . . . praise Your name For Your lovingkindness and Your truth; For You have magnified Your word above all Your name"* (Psalm 138:2).

What God has said in His word is even more important than His own name. So, His word is certainly high above matters of general revelation (the creation) and natural theology (reflective reasoning).

In this exalted word of truth, God's light shines forth to enlighten us and guide us and give us understanding.

> *"Your word is a lamp to my feet, and a light to my path"* (Psalm 119:105).

> *"The entrance of Your words gives light; It gives understanding to the simple"* (Psalm 119:130).

> *"In Your light we see light"* (Psalm 36:9).

Without this light from the Lord, our evaluation of the data around us would be shrouded in the darkness of our own misunderstandings.

Evaluating Everything by the Scriptures

Therefore, everything must be tried and evaluated by the light of the word of God.

"To the law and to the testimony! If they do not speak according to this word, it is because there is no light in them" (Isaiah 8:20).

In these days, many church leaders are not testing by the word of God the counseling approaches that they are using or recommending. Consequently, many leaders are compromising or displacing the message of the scriptures with their newly developing traditions of psychological integration. This distressing trend is a replication of the wrongdoing of the first century religious leadership. In Mark 7, Jesus sternly reprimanded them for their deadly folly, saying that they were . . .

". . . teaching as doctrines the commandments of men (verse 7) . . . *making the word of God of no effect through your tradition which you have handed down. And many such things you do"* (verse 13).

Instead of invalidating the Bible through allegiance to human theories, church leaders in particular, and all Christians in general, should be like the spiritually noble Bereans of Acts 17:11. They carefully measured every message by what the scriptures had to say.

"These were more noble-minded than those in Thessalonica, in that they received the word with all readiness, and searched the Scriptures daily to find out whether these things were so."

Since the Bereans were commended for checking on the reliability of the message of the Apostle Paul, should we not be even more diligent to examine by the word of God the theories of unredeemed psychological philosophers like Freud and Maslow and Skinner? Although these men possessed very impressive intellectual capabilities, they suffered from the incapacitating spiritual maladies described in Ephesians 4:17-18:

"This I say, therefore, and testify in the Lord, that you should no longer walk as the rest of the Gentiles walk, in the futility of their mind, having their understanding darkened, being alienated from the life of God, because of the ignorance that is in them, because of the hardening of their heart."

Why would the people of God ever want to integrate into their lives and ministries the defective speculations of those who not only had futile minds and darkened understanding but were alienated from God's life (and light)? Furthermore, along with spiritual ignorance, their hearts were hardened toward God!

The Crucial Flaw in This Cliché

When all is said and done, the primary fallacy in the "all-truth-is-God's-truth" cliché is the way it ignores or violates Jesus' teaching concerning the exact kind of truth that can be trusted to effectively change lives for God's purposes. Remember these words of Jesus that we considered earlier.

> *"Then Jesus said to those Jews who believed Him, 'If you abide in My word, you are My disciples indeed. And you shall know the truth, and the truth shall make you free' "* (John 8:31-32).

> *"Sanctify them by Your truth; Your word is truth"* (John 17:17).

Jesus did not send His followers off to search for truth any place that they might discover it. He did not tell them to be on the lookout for life-changing truths hidden within the writings of the learned thinkers among the family of man. No, He made it clear to all who would follow Him that the truth that changes lives, liberating and sanctifying them, is the truth of the word of God. In order for us to counsel His way, God wants us to rely wholly upon the truth of His word.

Warning about Counterfeits

Across the country and overseas, people

have often asked if it is necessary to specifi-cally warn about the dangers of the counter-feit truth propagated through psychological theory. Some people have suggested that it would be sufficient to approach this problem the way bankers are said to guard against counterfeit money. The story goes that bank tellers are given such a thorough exposure to real currency that they can notice any counter-feits in an instant. The implication for coun-seling is that all we need to do is instruct God's people sufficiently in the ways that His word lays out for proper counseling. Then we would all be automatically alert to any counterfeit psychological intrusions.

Well, the primary thrust of the word of God is to accentuate the realities of any subject that the scriptures address. However, the Bible consistently adds clear descriptive warnings about the very counterfeits that we should be guarding against. For example, in Matthew 15:11 Jesus proclaims this message of truth:

> *"Not what goes into the mouth defiles a man; but what comes out of the mouth, this defiles a man."*

Then, soon after He added a very specific warning concerning counterfeit messages.

> *"Then Jesus said to them, 'Take heed and beware of the leaven of the Pharisees and the Sadducees' "* (Matthew 16:6).

If we desire to be prepared to counsel one another God's way, we not only need to give and receive instruction concerning what God has for us, but also we need to give warnings about the counterfeits proliferating all around us. The word of God stresses the genuine, but it also clearly identifies that which is false.

Conclusion

The basic means God uses in counseling His way is the **word of God**. This is a fundamental and irreplaceable fact. This truth is perfectly linked with our anchor truth that the Lord Himself is our Wonderful Counselor. He counsels us through His very own words. So, when we seek counsel, may we look to the word of God alone. When others seek counsel through us, may we point them to the word of God alone. This is how the Lord will bring to people the life-giving, life-changing, life-liberating, life-sustaining truth that is universally needed.

"And I will pray the Father, and He will give you another Helper, that He may abide with you forever, even the Spirit of truth." — John 14:16-17

Chapter 5
The Holy Spirit in Counseling

The scriptures clearly establish **God's word** as the means to bring His counsel into our lives. The second means that God uses is inextricably interwoven with the first, and that is **the work of the Holy Spirit**. The use of the Bible in counseling does not depend upon human understanding or human ability to make the principles of the scriptures work properly. Rather, the Holy Spirit is available to minister to us and through us in these areas.

Another Helper Promised

In John 14:16-17, Jesus spoke of the Holy Spirit in terms that carry significance for the present subject:

> *"And I will pray the Father, and He will give you another Helper, that He may abide with you forever, even the Spirit of truth, whom the world cannot receive, because it neither sees Him nor knows Him; but you know Him, for He dwells with you and will be in you."*

When Jesus spoke these words, He was about to leave the disciples to return to His Father. The disciples were saddened by this announcement. Jesus had been their Teacher, their Master, their Helper, their Wonderful Counselor. So, He comforted them with the assurance that the Father would give them another Helper. This promised Helper would in essence be just like the previous one, because He also would be God.

A somewhat awkward, but accurate, translation of the term for Helper would be "one called alongside to help." That is what Jesus had been to the disciples when He was with them. Now, the Holy Spirit would carry on this type of ministry in their lives as one who would dwell within them and help them along their pathway through life.

This word contains some meaningful insights for true biblical counseling. Although we will look at it more extensively later, a brief comment will be useful at this time. This term, "one called alongside to help," here depicting the Holy Spirit, is one of two New Testament words sometimes translated in newer versions as Counselor. After Jesus, the Wonderful Counselor, ascended back to glory, the Holy Spirit would be sent by the Father to continue the divine counseling ministry of the Son.

This term is often translated Comforter, because providing comfort is so characteristic of being "one called along side to help." Offering a counsel of comfort is one of the two fundamental types of counseling we should be ready to give. The other is a counsel of confrontation. More will be furnished on both of these themes in the chapter on Church-Life.

The Spirit of Truth

In John 16:13, Jesus elaborates upon the ministry of the Holy Spirit:

> *"But when He, the Spirit of Truth, comes, He will guide you into all the truth"* (NASB).

Notice the title, the *"Spirit of Truth,"* given here to describe the Holy Spirit. How perfectly this title fits our context of God's means in counseling. God uses the truth of His word to impact lives, and the One who delivers this impact is called the Spirit of Truth. This One now lives in, and works through, the followers of the Lord Jesus Christ.

The One who inspired the truth recorded in the word of God is the Spirit of Truth. The Spirit of Truth is also the One who brings truth to bear upon people's lives. The Holy Spirit is absolutely indispensable to counseling God's way. Biblical counseling is not accomplished merely by having someone read or quote something from the word of God. The Holy Spirit is to be the motivating, instructing, convicting, transforming agent in every counseling situation. We must counsel in the same manner that all of ministry is to be done, *"in the newness of the Spirit and not in the oldness of the letter"* (Romans 7:6). This contrast is a matter of life and death, spiritually speaking, *"for the letter kills, but the Spirit gives life"* (2 Corinthians 3:6).

Our Guide into All the Truth

God intends to change lives through the power of the truth that is in His word. The Holy Spirit is given to guide us into this truth: *"He will guide you into all the truth."* The Spirit must direct us throughout the word of God as we read it and study it, and as we minister it to others. He alone unfolds and applies all of the scriptures, including those particular portions that we may have a special timely need to consider.

Things Freely Given by God

1 Corinthians 2:12-13 offers more powerful reasons why the Holy Spirit must be totally involved in the counseling ministry:

"Now we have received, not the spirit of the world, but the Spirit who is from God, that we might know the things that have been freely given to us by God. These things we also speak, not in words which man's wisdom teaches but which the Holy Spirit teaches, comparing spiritual things with spiritual."

We who are believers in the Lord Jesus Christ have not received the spirit of the world. The spirit of the world refers to the human wisdom of natural, unredeemed humanity. This earthly wisdom produces the ways of the world, including all of their values, goals, methodologies, theories, and resources. These very matters create so many of the prevailing counseling needs. On the other hand, we have received the Spirit who is from God, who meets all of these counseling needs.

One of the reasons we have received the Spirit is that we may know the things freely given to us by God. These are the divine resources of God's grace, imparted to us at His expense. These unlimited spiritual provisions are now ours in Christ. These heavenly riches are what we are to live on, grow in, and serve from, and then offer to others in His name. These are the things people need in counseling. We come to understand these realities by the revealing work of the Spirit of God, unfolding them to us through the word of God.

Consider what most people really need to find as they seek counseling. They need the forgiveness offered by Jesus Christ. They need the new life that is only available by God's grace. They need a love found in the Lord alone, a love which they could never deserve. They need hope and strength and peace and comfort. They need God to work in them to will and to do of His good pleasure. Well, these are *"the things that have been freely given to us by God."* Much of the biblical ministry of counseling has to do with speaking to people about these gracious gifts of God that are available to work in their lives.

Speaking of Things Freely Given

"These things we also speak" tells us to proclaim these wonderful things that God's grace provides. Sadly, the church of the Lord has become so intimidated by the world and its counseling theories and its psychotherapeutic systems that we too often think that we have nothing to say. After all, the world has all of those advanced educational degrees that

supposedly contain such deep insight into the heart of mankind. So, the church either sends searching and needy people into the world for help, or we try to bring the exalted wisdom of the world into the church. Instead, we should be speaking of the freely given things of God as the Lord intends.

Words Taught by the Holy Spirit

However, as we are speaking of these uniquely provided gifts of God's grace, we are to use the kind of words that the Lord has chosen. We are to speak, *"not in words which man's wisdom teaches but which the Holy Spirit teaches."* Increasingly, the Lord's people use the vocabulary of the world when speaking about man's problems and needed solutions. Now the church sounds just like the world speaking of dysfunctionalism, co-dependency, victimization, and self-esteem. Such terminology was not derived from biblical studies. These terms and concepts came from the humanistic theoreticians of the world. They are from man's wisdom, not from the teaching of the Holy Spirit.

We are to speak in words *"which the Holy Spirit teaches."* Perhaps we have forgotten that God has a great vocabulary. In fact, it is incomparable. When the Lord addresses man's needs and the necessary remedies, He uses divine terms that contain heavenly precision and supernatural hope. To describe man's problems, God uses words like sin, separation, bondage, death, alienation, condemnation, and judgment. God's remedies are explained in terms like conviction, repentance, confession, conversion, and salvation. To unfold the path of wholeness, He uses concepts like justification, sanctification, glorification, identification, dedication, and transformation.

In comparison to these heavenly, life-giving, life-changing words from God, man's earthly concepts are anemic and lifeless. May we minister the wisdom of God, not the wisdom of man. This is another reason that psychological theory falls so far short of what is needed when ministering to people. It speaks in words taught by mere human wisdom.

Comparing Spiritual with Spiritual

One of the reasons that we must counsel in Holy Spirit terms is that the Spirit compares *"spiritual things with spiritual."* The wisdom of man compares fleshly things with fleshly. When the church attempts to integrate psychological theories with biblical truths, the result is at best a comparing of fleshly things with spiritual. This becomes the proverbial impossibility of mixing water and oil.

The Spirit of God combines spiritual with spiritual. He creates spiritual life where there was spiritual death. He offers spiritual solutions to spiritual problems. He brings spiritual strength for spiritual weakness. He shines spiritual light where there was spiritual darkness. He provides spiritual liberty where there was spiritual bondage. He extends spiritual insight where there was spiritual confusion. Whatever the situation, the Spirit wants to bring spiritual to bear on spiritual. When this occurs in our personal ministry, godly biblical counseling can really take place.

UMBRELLA CLICHÉ #5: "Life's problems are too complex today to be using only the Bible and the Holy Spirit."

This umbrella cliché often arises at this point. It usually develops in this manner. The Bible is affirmed as good, and the Holy Spirit may even be acknowledged as important. However, life's problems are described as far more complex today than in "the Bible days." Consequently, they say the Bible is not enough for today, and the Holy Spirit is no longer sufficient. Many people have accepted that reasoning. Therefore, even God's people are out seeking after so-called "contemporary wisdom" and "up-to-date truth."

Have we forgotten that the author of the word of God is "I AM"? He is the eternal one. He does not get old or out of style. His pronouncements are not fads that pass away.

Even if we grant that life has become increasingly more complex and difficult to live, this does not mean that God's wisdom is inadequate. Considering the infinite measures of divine understanding, nothing is too complicated for the Holy Spirit.

Those who use this cliché to justify the use of psychological theories in the ministry of the church are inferring that God allowed insufficiencies in His word. Further, these "heavenly oversights" are now being remedied by godless, humanistic thinkers like Sigmund Freud and Carl Jung and Abraham Maslow and B. F. Skinner and others. May the Lord forgive us for selling His word so short and for not trusting in the work of His Spirit. In addition, may He awaken us to see how we are drifting from Him and His word.

Conclusion

Along with **His word**, the second basic means God uses in getting His counsel into our lives is **the Holy Spirit**. True biblical counseling cannot take place without the full involvement of the Spirit of Truth. So when we are looking for counsel from the Lord, or being used to share His counsel with others, we need to depend upon the Spirit to lead us and guide us into the truth of His word. Likewise, when others come to us for godly counsel, we want to urge them to put their hope in the work of the Holy Spirit to ensure any spiritual benefit for their lives.

"For this reason we also, since the day we heard it, do not cease to pray for you, and to ask that you may be filled with the knowledge of His will in all wisdom and spiritual understanding." — Colossians 1:9

Chapter 6
Prayer in Counseling

Along with **the word of God** and the **Spirit of God**, the third means that the Lord uses to make His counsel available is **prayer**. Since the Lord is our Wonderful Counselor, and the counsel of His word unfolds by the Holy Spirit, prayer is essential in counseling God's way. Prayer expresses our desire for, and dependence upon, the work of God in our lives. The necessary work of the Spirit takes place in prayerful, seeking hearts.

Praying from God's Word

Praying that is based solely upon the content of God's word is the safest and most effective praying of all, because God's will is revealed in His word.

"Now this is the confidence that we have in Him, that if we ask anything according to His will, He hears us. And if we know that He hears us, whatever we ask, we know that we have the petitions that we have asked of Him" (1 John 5:14-15).

In light of such truth, perhaps our wisest praying would be patterned after the very prayers of godly men in the word of God. There are two such prayers in the scriptures by the Apostle Paul that have special import for those who are seeking or giving counsel.

Knowing God's Will

One of these prayers is found in Colossians 1:9:

"For this reason we also, since the day we heard it, do not cease to pray for you, and to ask that you may be filled with the knowledge of His will in all wisdom and spiritual understanding."

This prayer is about lives being filled with knowing God's will. The knowledge petitioned for here is that which comes from God's wisdom and understanding being imparted to man. Since so much of the counseling ministry involves people seeking to know the will of God, this is an outstanding prayer both for those seeking counsel as well as those giving counsel.

There are various reasons why such seekers do not readily find God's will. Most of these reasons are related to two general warnings that James gave. Some people do not even ask the Lord for what is needed. Other people ask God, but for reasons of fleshly indulgence.

> *"You do not have because you do not ask. You ask and do not receive, because you ask amiss, that you may spend it on your pleasures"* (James 4:2-3).

So, some people fail to seek the Lord because they get distracted by a vain pursuit of man's wisdom, thereby becoming preoccupied with human opinions and earthly advice. Others get side-tracked by presumption, wrongly assuming that they fully understand what God's will for them would be. Still others take their request for knowing God's will directly to the Lord Himself, yet are driven only by self-serving motivations.

The remedy for these exercises in futility is to be crying out to our Wonderful Counselor that He would cause us to *"be filled with the knowledge of His will in all wisdom and spiritual understanding."*

Knowing God Himself

The other prayer in the word that has special significance for the subject of biblical counseling is found in Ephesians 1:17. This is a prayer that *"the God of our Lord Jesus Christ, the Father of glory, may give to you a spirit of wisdom and of revelation in the knowledge of Him."* This verse summarizes the greatest common need that we possess. It is the need for more of the knowledge of God.

This obviously applies to those who are in the world, those who have no personal saving knowledge of God. Their number one priority need is to get to know Him through the saving work of the Lord Jesus Christ. However, for those who are already walking in a saving relationship with the Lord, their foremost pressing need is still to get to know Him better.

For Those Who Don't Know God

Let's apply this truth first to those who do not know the Lord in a saving way. Many people searching for counsel and direction in life have not yet found forgiveness of sins and new life through Jesus Christ. They are often struggling with problems, difficulties, and challenges for which they have no sufficient answers. When such individuals come to churches or Christian friends for help, they need above all else to receive counsel that gives them an opportunity to meet the Lord through His saving grace. Their greatest need is not how to deal with a troubled teenager, or how to control their temper, or how to respond to stress on the job. They need to get to know the Lord. Then, the Lord can begin to work in all of their other lesser needs.

The Gospel and Meeting the Lord

The initial saving encounter with the Lord comes through the gospel of Jesus Christ. The gospel is the "good news" that Jesus, who was the Word of God and the Son of God, came to earth as a man.

> *"In the beginning was the Word, and the Word was with God, and the Word was God. And the Word became flesh and dwelt among us, and we beheld His glory, the glory as of the only begotten of the Father, full of grace and truth"*
> (John 1:1, 14).

This Jesus died on the cross for the sins of the world and was raised from the dead to provide victory over sin and death.

> *"Moreover, brethren, I declare to you the gospel which I preached to you . . . that Christ died for our sins according to the Scriptures, and that He was buried, and that He rose again the third day according to the Scriptures. O Death, where is your sting? O Hades (grave), where is your victory? But thanks be to God, who*

gives us the victory through our Lord Jesus Christ" (1 Corinthians 15:1, 3, 55, 57).

Thus, this same Jesus brings spiritual new birth into the family of God for all who believe in Him, receiving Him as Lord and Savior.

"He came to His own, and His own did not receive Him. But as many as received Him, to them He gave the right to become children of God, to those who believe in His name: who were born, not of blood, nor of the will of the flesh, nor of the will of man, but of God" (John 1:11-13).

" Jesus answered and said to him, 'Most assuredly, I say to you, unless one is born again, he cannot see the kingdom of God' " (John 3:3).

Thus, the loving grace of God provides forgiveness and eternal life to all who repent of their sins and put their trust in the Lord Jesus for salvation.

"Jesus came to Galilee, preaching the gospel of the kingdom of God, and saying, 'The time is fulfilled, and the kingdom of God is at hand. Repent, and believe in the gospel' " (Mark 1:14).

"For God so loved the world that He gave His only begotten Son, that whoever believes in Him should not perish but have everlasting life" (John 3:16).

For Those Who Do Know God

Now, let's apply this ultimate priority matter of knowing God to those who have already begun a saving relationship with the Lord Jesus Christ. Their greatest need is still to get to know the Lord. Yes, they have met Him and have started to walk with Him. Developing this relationship in a deeper and more intimate manner is the goal now.

Consider how a deepening acquaintanceship with God affects every area of a person's life. Getting to know the Lord in an increasing way means that we will understand more and more fully who He is, how He thinks, what He has done for us, what He can do in and through us, and much, much more. Such knowledge of God impacts the things that people face daily.

If someone is tormented by fear, knowing more of the Lord's protecting power replaces that fear with security in Him. If a person is immobilized by confusion, knowing more of the Lord's wisdom replaces that confusion with direction from Him. If anyone is overwhelmed by his own inadequacies, knowing the spiritual resources available to us through Christ can bring hope and peace. Likewise, if an individual is puffed up in pride, knowing the meekness and lowliness of the Lord Jesus produces the humility and dependence that pleases Him.

On the other hand, if someone is exhilarated by a stirring vision of godly Christian service, he needs a growing knowledge of the Lord in order to evaluate the vision, as well as to see it properly fulfilled. Also, if a person is gifted and fruitful, knowing the convicting and guarding ministry of the Holy Spirit will remind him of the heavenly source from which all of that spiritual blessing flows.

In each and every situation of life and pilgrimage, getting to know the Lord better is our greatest need. There is not a need, a challenge, a heartache, a hope, a dream, or an opportunity that cannot be properly impacted by a greater knowledge of the Lord.

Helping others to know the Lord better could be a wonderful, primary goal for all of our counseling and personal ministry. If we were simply dedicated to helping everyone who comes our way to know more of Him, everyone we ministered to would be helped greatly. Consequently, this prayer in Ephesians 1:17 can be an invaluable way to pray and to urge others to pray: *"that the God of our Lord Jesus Christ, the Father of glory, may give to you a spirit of wisdom and of revelation in the knowledge of Him."*

Overall Place of Prayer

Beyond these two profound prayers of knowing God and being filled with the knowledge of His will, it is good to be reminded of the overall place of prayer in Christian life and ministry. God's word makes it clear in so many places that prayer is to be a part of everything that comes our way.

> *"Trust in Him at all times, you people;*
> *Pour out your heart before Him"*
> (Psalm 62:8).

> *"Then He spoke a parable to them, that men always ought to pray and not lose heart"* (Luke 18:1).

> *"Praying always with all prayer and sup- plication in the Spirit, being watchful to this end with all perseverance and supplication for all the saints"* (Ephesians 6:18).

> *"Be anxious for nothing, but in everything by prayer and supplication, with thanks- giving, let your requests be made known to God"* (Philippians 4:6).

> *"Pray without ceasing"* (1 Thessalonians 5:17).

Clearly, prayer is to have a constant place in all that we experience. May our counseling and discipleship ministries be permeated with the habit of prayer.

Conclusion

Thus, **prayer, God's word,** and **the work of the Holy Spirit** bring the Lord's counsel into lives. Without prayer, counseling can never be what God intended. Through the years, I have marveled and anguished over the testimonies of those who sought help in the so-called Christian counseling centers and clinics and too often found prayer neglected altogether. May we cry out to the Lord to prevent this in our personal work and counseling ministry. May those who seek help from us find us to be people of prayer, and may they also become people of prayer themselves.

"Blessed be the God and Father of our Lord Jesus Christ, the Father of mercies and God of all comfort, who comforts us in all our tribulation, that we may be able to comfort those who are in any trouble, with the comfort with which we ourselves are comforted by God."
— 2 Corinthians 1:3-4

Chapter 7
Church-Life in Counseling

We have considered three of the basic means that the Lord uses to get His counsel to us: the **word of God**, **the Holy Spirit**, and **prayer**. We will look more at each of these in the chapter on "The Counseling Situation," which examines biblically that moment when we are actually sitting down "one on one" with another person. However, there is an essential fourth area, **church-life**, that warrants careful attention as well.

Church-Life Described

Church-life refers to Christians living together as the family of God, walking in the relationships and drawing on the resources that we have available as the people of the Lord. This matter of living together in the body of Christ is a critical part of counseling God's way. Colossians 3:12-17 is a magnificent, concise depiction of this life, which includes a call to be counseling one another:

"Therefore, as the elect of God, holy and beloved, put on tender mercies, kindness, humbleness of mind, meekness, longsuffering; bearing with one another, and forgiving one another, if anyone has a complaint against another; even as Christ forgave you, so you also must do. But above all these things put on love, which is the bond of perfection. And let the peace of God rule in your hearts, to which also you were called in one body; and be thankful. Let the word of Christ dwell in you richly in all wisdom, teaching and admonishing one another in psalms and hymns and spiritual songs, singing with grace in your hearts to the Lord. And whatever you do in word or deed, do all in the name of the Lord Jesus, giving thanks to God the Father through Him."

Note some of the key phrases that establish this as a picture of life in the church, the body of Christ: *"the elect of God . . . holy and beloved . . . as Christ forgave you . . . you were called in one body."* This clearly describes the chosen, set apart, dearly loved, forgiven family of God. Also, notice some of the terms that indicate how the church is to live and function together: *"one another* (appearing three times) . . . *bond of perfection . . . the peace of God . . . the word of Christ . . . all in the name of the Lord Jesus."* Such terms portray a setting in which believers are touching each other's lives by love, kindness, patience, forgiveness, and unity, while all are being touched by God's word, His peace, and His presence. This is the spiritual environment in which God has ordained that counseling is to occur.

Counseling by Confrontation

In verse 16, the phrase *"admonishing one another"* has great implications for the biblical counseling ministry. The word that is translated as "admonishing" could also be rendered as "counseling." In fact, some versions of the Bible translate it at times as counseling. The original word in the verb form is "noutheteo." Dr. Jay Adams, a gifted biblical counselor and renowned biblical linguist, used this term to create the expression "Nouthetic Counseling." This aspect of biblical counseling has to do with **confrontation**, bringing people face to face with the truth of God's word. Such admonitions thereby produce a divine accountability to the authority of God's word and its declared consequences.

Counseling One Another

Notice further the inclusion of the phrase **"one another."** There are many one another ministries listed in the word of God for **all** of the family of God. Some are given right here in our present Colossians passage; namely, forgiving one another, bearing with one another, teaching and admonishing (or, counseling) one another. Christians are to be "counseling one another." Counseling God's way is a ministry for all of God's people to some degree. It is a ministry of mutuality and reciprocity, each to the other.

Without question, the extent to which each of God's people will be involved in counseling others will vary widely, depending on factors like gift, calling, maturity, equipping, and availability. Nonetheless, all are potentially included in the biblical design for counseling.

God has arranged for counseling to take place in the church-life setting. The ministry of counseling was not designed to take place in some isolated professional clinic or office. Even so-called Christian counseling clinics generally have two major shortcomings. First, they are separated from the full measure of life in the body of Christ. Second, such clinics are too often committed to integrating the corrupted psychological theories of man with the pure word of God.

Counseling from God's perspective is not

for the professional psychological elite. It is to be shared by every Christian, while relating together as the family of God. We are to counsel each other. None of us has all of God's answers, but all of us have something of spiritual value to contribute to one another. Furthermore, we can all grow in learning how to minister to each other.

One Key Aspect of Counseling One Another

In 2 Corinthians 1:3-4, there is a beautiful picture of one of the ways that we are all are able to counsel one another:

> *"Blessed be the God and Father of our Lord Jesus Christ, the Father of mercies and God of all comfort, who comforts us in all our tribulation, that we may be able to comfort those who are in any trouble, with the comfort with which we ourselves are comforted by God."*

Notice the emphatic recurrence of this inviting term, "**comfort**." This word in the original is from the verb "parakaleo." This is one of the two Greek terms that some versions translate at times as "counseling" (the other, as noted earlier, is "noutheteo"). "Parakaleo" speaks of being called alongside to offer help and encouragement.

A noun form of this word ("paracletos") has produced a transliterated English term,

"Paraclete," that many use when referring to the Holy Spirit. Various versions translate this as Comforter or Helper or Counselor in certain instances. The Holy Spirit is the One whom the Father has called to come alongside and help His people and enable them to comfort and counsel one another.

The Source of All True Comfort

The God of all comfort is the primary subject of these verses. All true comfort must be of God, or it is merely temporal, fleshly, man-centered, earth-bound comfort. Our God of all valid and effective comfort is the one who comforts us in all our afflictions, all of our pressures and difficulties and impossibilities. One of the reasons He comforts us is so that we may be able to comfort others. Certainly, God comforts us, because He has compassion upon us. However, He also has a bigger picture in mind. He intends us to pass on His comfort to others.

Comfort for Any Difficulty

Sometimes we think we cannot give a person any counsel in their particular affliction, since we have never faced precisely what they are going through. Yes, it is wonderful when God comforts us through someone who has experienced exactly what we are encountering. However, that is not the only ministry of comfort that one believer can offer another. If we have been afflicted in any manner and have found comfort from God, we can tell any other afflicted person about that comfort we received. The God of all comfort uses our testimony to remind them of the comforting source. This encourages them to look to Him, that they might also be comforted by Him.

Confrontation and Comfort, Law and Grace

Again, God has ordained that counseling is to take place within the context of church-life. Also, we have seen that this counsel from God will include **confrontation** (from the term "noutheteo"). Subsequently, we have come across a different term that involves counsel by **comfort** (from "parakaleo"). The entire scope of biblical counseling is encompassed by these two terms. Many people seeking counsel need to be confronted by the standards, demands, and consequences of God's word. Others need to be comforted by the provisions, promises, and assurances of the word of God. Everyone seeking counsel needs to receive one or the other of these, or an appropriate combination of the two.

In order to understand whether a person should receive confrontation or comfort, we must consider the characteristics, purposes, and uses of **law** and **grace**. We will see that the law of God is related to counseling by confrontation, while the grace of God is related to counseling by comfort.

Counseling from God's Law

The character of the law of God is holiness, as reflected in Leviticus 19:1-4:

> *"And the LORD spoke to Moses, saying, 'Speak to all the congregation of the children of Israel, and say to them: 'You shall be holy, for I the LORD your God am holy. Every one of you shall revere his mother and his father, and keep My Sabbaths: I am the LORD your God. Do not turn to idols, nor make for yourselves molded gods: I am the LORD your God'."*

Here, amidst various commands from the law, the Lord says, *"You shall be holy, for I the LORD your God am holy."* The law of God reveals the holy character of God, and it demands that God's people walk in the path of holiness depicted in its commands.

The great purpose of the law of God is to show us what sin is all about, thereby making us accountable to God. Then, it can tutor us to Christ for His forgiveness and new life.

> *"Now we know that whatever the law says, it says . . . that every mouth may be stopped, and all the world may become guilty before God. Therefore by the deeds of the law no flesh will be justified in His*

sight, for by the law is the knowledge of sin" (Romans 3:19-20).

"Therefore the law was our tutor to bring us to Christ, that we might be justified by faith" (Galatians 3:24).

Also, one of the vital uses of the law of God is to confront rebellious and willful hearts.

"But we know that the law is good if one uses it lawfully, knowing this: that the law is not made for a righteous person, but for the lawless and insubordinate, for the ungodly and for sinners, for the unholy and profane" (1 Timothy 1:8-9).

Whenever we are counseling those who are indulging in sin or rebellion against the ways of God, the Lord will primarily want us to confront them with His law. This will give them the opportunity to repent of their spiritual insubordination and to humble themselves before the Lord, both for initial salvation, as well as for renewed progress in the faith.

Counseling from God's Grace

The character of the grace of God is love, as reflected in Romans 5:1, 2 and 8:

"Therefore, having been justified by faith, we have peace with God through our Lord Jesus Christ, through whom also we have access by faith into this grace in which we

stand . . . but God demonstrates His own love toward us, in that while we were still sinners, Christ died for us."

Here, the work of God's grace for salvation demonstrates His great, sacrificial love. The grace of God reveals the loving character of God, and it encourages people to trust in the one who loves them so greatly.

The highest purpose of the grace of God is to restore us to the life of godliness that the law so perfectly proclaims and demands, but which the law cannot provide.

"For the law made nothing perfect; on the other hand, there is the bringing in of a better hope, through which we draw near to God . . . For it is good that the heart be established by grace" (Hebrews 7:19 and 13:9).

That better hope is the life-giving grace of God, which develops deep within our hearts an intimate, life-changing relationship with our glorious God of infinite love.

One of the great uses of the grace of God is to comfort hearts that are humble, meek, and receptive.

"But He gives more grace. Therefore He says: 'God resists the proud, but gives grace to the humble' " (James 4:6).

Whenever we are counseling those who

are broken and humble before the Lord, He will primarily want us to comfort them with His grace. This will give them the hope and encouragement they need to trust in Him and His measureless resources, which are able to produce the life that God desires.

Thus, everyone seeking counsel needs to receive counsel by law or counsel by grace, or an appropriate combination of the two. These are the categories of growth and counsel that the Lord develops in our lives, as we minister to one another in church-life. We will examine many aspects of this process in the chapters that lie ahead.

Conclusion

So, the fourth fundamental means that God employs in bringing His counsel into lives is **church-life**, wherein God's people share life together in Christ. This is the setting that God has committed to use.

Summary of Sections One and Two

What has been said thus far about "A Biblical Perspective on Counseling" and "God's Basic Means in Counseling" could be summarized in the following extended statement.

Counseling God's Way consists of:
- the comprehensive, all-sufficient wisdom and knowledge of **Jesus, our**

Wonderful Counselor,

- given to us for **discipleship** and **sanctification,**
- through the life-giving, life-changing, life-liberating, life-sustaining truth of **the word of God,**
- by the full involvement of **the Holy Spirit,** the Spirit of Truth,
- involving **prayer** from trusting, seeking hearts,
- all in the context of the Lord's love being shared in the relationships and **"one another"** ministries of **Christ's church,**
- while being alert and careful to avoid the **philosophical wisdom of this world** and the **resources of the self-life.**

Counseling God's way is not getting ideas from the experts of the world in psychological theory. Rather, it is putting our hope in the Lord and using His ordained means of counseling. Let's ask God to show us if the counsel that we receive and the counsel that we give fits His pattern. If so, thank God and press ahead in it. If not, let's allow the Lord to adjust our counseling to His will. Also, may we pray for all in the church world to do the same.

SECTION THREE

Equipping Counselors

At this point, we enter into another major segment of our study in counseling God's way. This section on **"Equipping Counselors"** builds upon the biblical fact that the counseling ministry is designed for all of God's people. We will examine who should be involved in the counseling ministry. We will also look at how all Christians can prepare for such service. Then, we will explore vital spiritual truths that provide more preparation for counseling. Finally, we will consider some biblical guidelines for all counseling situations, for those times when one believer sits down face-to-face to help one who seeks or needs direction.

Once again, this is a strategic area of study. Without this input from the word of God, the Lord's church is naturally inclined to think that most counseling should be referred to the experts who are trained in man's psychological wisdom. This section of study assures us that God's people can be equipped to offer His counsel to one another.

> "As far as I am concerned about you, my brothers, I am convinced that you are especially abounding in the highest goodness, richly supplied with perfect knowledge and competent to counsel one another."
> — Romans 15:14 [Williams]

Chapter 8
Who is to Do Counseling

Romans 15:14 will be our starting point for the important matter of **who is to do counseling**:

> *"Now I myself am confident concerning you, my brethren, that you also are full of goodness, filled with all knowledge, able also to admonish one another."*

Every Believer in General

This passage, and elsewhere in the word of God, makes it quite evident that **every believer in general** is to be involved in the counseling ministry. This verse contains the same phrase found in Colossians 3:16 concerning *"admonishing one another."* The original term is again from the verb "noutheteo," which can be rendered counseling. This statement by the Lord through the Apostle Paul is addressed to the "brethren," to all of the brothers and sisters of the family of God in the church at Rome. By application, it is for every Christian in any New Testament church, then or throughout the church age. Consequently, we have here an indication that all believers in general are to counsel one another.

Competent to Counsel

This raises the question of whether or not Christians are competent to counsel one another. The final portion of Romans 15:14 speaks directly to this matter: *"able also to admonish one another."* This phrase is translated in the Williams Translation of the New Testament as *"competent to counsel one another."* This is the passage from which Dr. Jay Adams took the title of his classic book on biblical counseling, called "Competent To Counsel," that was published in 1970. God pronounces all believers as potentially capable of giving godly counsel to one another.

Filled with Goodness and Knowledge

Fourteen and one-half chapters of Romans, proclaiming the person and work and provisions of the Lord Jesus Christ, have preceded this declaration of competency to counsel. Believers who grow in these revelations of the goodness of the Lord and the knowledge of God become increasingly and practically those who are thereby *"competent to counsel."* Such competency comes from drawing upon these wonderful resources available to all in Christ Jesus.

To some people, this assertion of general competency in counseling one another sounds only marginally acceptable. They think that this informal approach to helping each other might suffice in situations of minor need. However, what about the tough cases? This reasoning often concludes with the following cliché.

UMBRELLA CLICHÉ #6:
"We must always be prepared to send the difficult counseling cases to the psychologically trained experts, since they are the only ones who fully understand man and can thereby deal effectively with complex problems."

Yes, we should be ready to send the tough cases to the experts. However, it is essential that we realize from God's vantage point who the experts actually are.

God's Counseling Experts

The true experts in the family of God are not those who are psychologically trained in man's wisdom, hoping to understand man by studying human theories about man. Rather, they are the ones that God gifts, equips, and raises up in the unfolding process of church-life.

The Lord has a way to develop expert counselors among His family. Romans 12:6 and 8 gives insight into this provision:

> *"Having then gifts differing according to the grace that is given to us . . . he who exhorts, in exhortation . . . ."*

Verse six makes it clear that the context pertains to spiritual gifts. Part of the grace poured out upon us in Christ Jesus is the imparting of spiritual gifts. These gifts are divine enablings of the Holy Spirit, allowing us to function effectively in the characteristic manner that God has in mind for each of us individually.

The Spiritual Gift of Counseling

Verse 8 specifies one of these gifts as *"exhortation."* This word is from a verb that we have previously considered, "parakaleo." It is one of the two Greek terms that can be translated "counseling." The gift specified here would be (or, would include) the spiritual gift of counseling.

All of God's people in general are to be counseling one another. Some of God's people in particular have also been given the spiritual gift of counseling. They are the ones in the body of Christ sovereignly gifted by God to provide spiritual counseling in a distinctively proficient manner. They are the ones who are to become the Lord's experts in His family. All of us can and need to counsel others to some degree. However, for some, counseling will become their primary ministry, because they are supernaturally gifted by God to function in that capacity.

Maturing from Spiritual Meat

Spiritual gifting alone will not make a Christian an expert biblical counselor. There must also be that type of maturing spoken of in Hebrews 5:13-14:

> *"For everyone who partakes only of milk is unskilled in the word of righteousness, for he is a babe. But solid food* (i.e., meat) *belongs to those who are of full age* (i.e., mature), *that is, those who by reason of use have their senses exercised to discern both good and evil."*

Even those who are greatly gifted by the Lord to offer His counsel must also grow and mature spiritually, if they are going to use their gifts to their fullest potential. If they only feed on basic spiritual milk (such as, "Christ died for us"), they will remain babes in Christ.

Conversely, if they get into the meat of the word (such as, "Christ lives in us"), and then live by the truth of that solid food, their spiritual senses will be trained to minister with effective spiritual discernment. They will be able to help others to distinguish the difference between things which are of God or of the enemy, and between things which are of the Spirit or of the flesh.

This type of godly growth and development is what turns the gifted counselor into an effective "spiritual expert," one we can refer people to when the help we offered is insufficient. Some of these experts are in vocational leadership roles on church staffs. Others are not highly visible or obviously recognizable as counselors, because they function daily as educators or business men or grandparents. Yet, they are gifted by God to counsel with remarkable competency, and they are matured in Him to counsel with notable effectiveness. May the Lord raise up an army of such experts among us!

Medical Expertise

We will examine later the place of medical expertise, and the role it can fulfill in counseling those who are experiencing problems related to genuine physiological irregularities. However, even in situations that may involve the acceptable "common grace" use of medical science, we still want to be alert to avoid the influence of the philosophical input of psychological theory.

Increasing Usability for All Counselors

In addition to the general counseling competency that is available to all believers and the special gifting that is given to some, those who grow and develop in the following spiritual realities will be especially usable in the hands of the Wonderful Counselor.

Abiding in Christ

In John 15:4-5, Jesus spoke truth that has profound implications for our subject:

> *"Abide in Me, and I in you. As the branch cannot bear fruit of itself, unless it abides in the vine, neither can you, unless you abide in Me. I am the vine, you are the branches. He who abides in Me, and I in him, bears much fruit; for without Me you can do nothing."*

To the extent that Christians abide in Christ, their lives and their counseling ministry will both be richly enhanced. Jesus calls us all to abide in Him and allow Him to live in and through us. A physical branch cannot bear physical fruit unless it draws its life from the vine. Likewise, we who are spiritual branches cannot bear spiritual fruit unless we draw our life from Jesus, the vine.

What people need to hear when we counsel them is what the Lord alone can give them. They do not need what the branch can supply on its own. They need what is in the vine coming out through the life of the branch. The vine is the Wonderful Counselor. People seeking counsel from us need to find fruit in our lives that results from a dependent relationship with Christ.

We need to abide in Christ if we want much fruit in counseling. Apart from Him, we can do nothing in the realm of godly counseling. The more a child of God grows in the abiding life, looking to Christ for everything, resting in Him, trusting in Him, hoping in Him, the more will be the fruit he will bear in personal ministry to others.

Living by the Spirit

Just as abiding in Christ enriches the counseling ministry, so also does living by the Spirit. Galatians 5:22-23 and 25 speaks of such a life:

> *"But the fruit of the Spirit is love, joy, peace, longsuffering, kindness, goodness, faithfulness, gentleness, self-control . . . If we live in the Spirit, let us also walk in the Spirit."*

Love is so important when we are counseling one another. If we counsel with a love-
less heart, our counsel will be dead and
uncaring. We will easily become impatient or
unkind or lacking in gentleness or being out
of control. Where are we going to find the
love that we need? It is from the Spirit of
God. In fact, the primary fruit of the Spirit is
love. Actually, these other wonderful characteristics of the Spirit at work may simply be
various aspects of God's love working in our
lives. When we serve people with supernatural joy, peace, longsuffering, kindness, goodness, faithfulness, gentleness, and self-control,
their lives can be impacted mightily. We need
the fruit of the Spirit!

Such spiritual fruit develops in those who
live by the Spirit. Since we had to receive
spiritual life from the Holy Spirit in order to
be born again, let us walk daily in the path of
dependence. The entire life in Christ should
be undertaken by humble reliance upon the
guiding, energizing, and sustaining work of
the Holy Spirit. Fruitful biblical counseling
hinges on such a spiritual walk. It does not
hinge on psychological training in the intricacies of man's make-up, as man has attempted
to understand man. Counseling God's way
necessitates the presence of Christ-like fruit in
our lives, thereby impacting others who come
to us for help.

Living by the Word and by Prayer

Living by the word and by prayer also enhances our capacity to counsel as God intends. Both of these matters are addressed in one strategic verse, in John 15:7:

> *"If you abide in Me, and My words abide in you, you will ask what you desire, and it shall be done for you."*

This statement adds two other matters to the abiding life in Christ: the word of God and prayer. As we abide in Christ, God wants His words to abide in us, that is, dwell in and direct every area of our lives. As we regularly listen to the Lord in His word, this reality can develop in us. Then, our praying can rest upon this great promise: *"You will ask what you desire, and it shall be done for you."*

This pledge from God should not produce a carnal shopping list of earthly cravings. On the contrary, our prayer life must be continually guided by the word of God living in us. The more His word abides in us, the more our prayers will be controlled by His word. Characteristically, we will request what the word proclaims and provides. Thus, our personal ministry to others will be marked by answered prayers, according to the will of God.

Keeping Confidences

The keeping of confidences is another

character quality that increases our capacity to bring God's counsel to others. Proverbs 11:13 contains the insights that unfold this truth:

> *"A tale bearer reveals secrets, but he who is of a faithful spirit conceals a matter."*

In the counseling ministry you hear amazing things. You hear things sometimes that you almost wish you did not hear, because there is a spiritual responsibility for whatever is heard. Yet, there is a carnal, fleshly curiosity that wants to hear every possible detail of every testing or failure. In addition, there is often a temptation to share these secrets inappropriately with others.

It is clear from this scripture that God does not want us spreading around what we have learned in private conversation. This is what tale bearers do. Instead, He desires to form a faithful spirit in us. He wants to give us a steadfast, reliable, and trustworthy character that will keep confidence with people who open up their hearts to us. Such faithful integrity as a counselor will decidedly strengthen one's counseling ministry.

Sacrificing for Others

Willingness to sacrifice personally for the benefit of those in need is another factor that enriches a person's counseling ministry. 1 John 3:16 relates to this issue:

"By this we know love, because He laid down His life for us. And we also ought to lay down our lives for the brethren."

The love of God was ultimately shown in that Jesus Christ came and laid down His life on the cross for us. This sacrificial death for our sins was not only to secure our salvation, it was also an example for us to follow. We are to love as He loved. He loved sacrificially. We are to express the love of God by laying down our lives for the brethren. We are to give of ourselves for the benefit and blessing of others. We are to lay down our time, our energy, our interests.

Typically, opportunities to share the Lord's counsel with others arise at bothersome moments. If we are not willing to sacrifice our comfort and convenience, our personal ministry will be greatly impeded. Conversely, it will tend to flourish if we lovingly lay ourselves down for others.

Conclusion

The biblical mandate concerning **who is to counsel** is directed first to **every believer in general**. Furthermore, it is particularly designed for those Christians who have been spiritually gifted by the Lord for more extensive personal ministry. Moreover, for every believer in general, and for the gifted in particular, all can have their usefulness greatly enhanced if they are abiding in Christ, living by His Spirit, living by His word, living by prayer, keeping confidences, and sacrificing for others.

"And He Himself gave some to be apostles, some prophets, some evangelists, and some pastors and teachers, for the equipping of the saints for the work of ministry, for the edifying of the body of Christ."
— Ephesians 4:11-12

Chapter 9
Equipping for Counseling Ministry

Being equipped for personal ministry is appropriate for **every believer**, since all Christians are called to participate in the counseling ministry. Likewise, those who are particularly gifted by God for substantial involvement in counseling will also benefit from the process of being equipped to better serve Him. The Lord has provided such a plan for all of His people.

Equipping by Church Leaders

Ephesians 4:11-12 sets forth the basic arrangement that God has instituted for equipping us for the ministries to which He has called us:

123

"And He Himself gave some to be apostles, some prophets, some evangelists, and some pastors and teachers, for the equipping of the saints for the work of ministry, for the edifying of the body of Christ."

This is the general equipping pattern for all of the family of God. The Lord gives to the church various people gifted in leadership. One of the primary functions for leaders in the church is the *"equipping of the saints for the work of ministry."* Equipping speaks of being trained for service, being outfitted for battle.

As church leaders teach us God's word and exemplify Christian ministry, they are equipping us to minister in His name. In order to be more used of God in ministry, we are to be consistently associated with the lives and ministries of the leaders of the church. God wants to use them to feed us, guide us, and prepare us for more service in His kingdom.

Ministry for All Believers

In the equipping of the saints, remember that "saints" refers to all Christians, not to some religiously elite group or category. Too often in the church world, we think of ministry as being exclusively for those who have "fully arrived spiritually" or are in vocational Christian work, so-called "full-time ministry." Such thinking is foreign to the word of God.

124

If we are believers in Jesus Christ, we are called to serve in a variety of ministries.

Every follower of the Lord is called to minister in worship, praise, and prayer, all directed toward God. Each member of the body of Christ is to minister to other members of the church, as noted previously in the "one another ministries" (including counseling one another). In addition, all Christians are commissioned to the ministry of witnessing to the unsaved. Furthermore, the Lord has given all of His people spiritual gifts, which define and develop our ministry specializations. In each of these categories, God wants to equip us unto fruitfulness and effectiveness.

Equipping One Another

Church leaders are not the only ones who are to apply themselves to equipping believers for ministry. Actually, all of us are to be involved in this process, each of us helping the other. The scriptures present this frequently overlooked fact in various places.

> *"Therefore let us pursue the things which make for peace and the things by which one may edify another"* (Romans 14:19).

> *"Let each of us please his neighbor for his good, leading to edification"* (Romans 15:2).

> *"Therefore comfort each other and edify*

one another, just as you also are doing"
(1 Thessalonians 5:11).

All of the one another ministries set forth in the word of God can contribute to the process of equipping each other. The one cited above, "edifying one another," is one of the more obvious. Edifying and building up each other is what the Lord intends. This involves helping others to learn, grow, and mature. This includes assisting others in facing difficulties properly, making biblical decisions, developing discernment, and establishing priorities.

Edifying one another is part of what God ordains for all of us in order to become more equipped for service unto Him. Some of the wonder and simplicity of this biblical approach to reciprocal training is its flexibility and versatility. Although it can obviously take place at a Home Discipleship Study, it can also occur at a church picnic. While it certainly can happen at a Sunday Morning Worship Service, it can also transpire on a mountain hike as well. Whereas it can definitely unfold in a School of Ministry class, it can even operate at a family reunion.

The concluding point in equipping one another is that it not only outfits us more for all ministry in general, but it also increases our effectiveness for the counseling ministry in particular.

Equipping through God's Word

As we are being equipped by church leaders, by one another, and by our own private spiritual regimen of prayer and devotions, equipping through the word of God must be seen as central and irreplaceable. 2 Timothy 3:16-17 establishes this compelling truth:

> *"All Scripture is given by inspiration of God, and is profitable for doctrine, for reproof, for correction, for instruction in righteousness, that the man of God may be complete, thoroughly equipped for every good work."*

The Inspiration and Ability of the Scriptures

All of the scriptures are inspired by God. This means that every word is literally "God-breathed." Even though God used the personalities and vocabularies of the prophets and the apostles, His human instruments, He nonetheless stated through their writings exactly what He intended to communicate. Consequently, the Bible has the divinely-ordained ability to do all that God sent it to do. Whenever the Holy Spirit is allowed to use the scriptures in our lives, indispensable spiritual processes take place within us.

Doctrine, Reproof, Correction, Instruction in Righteousness

One of the greatest needs that every person has is to receive an accurate description of God and His path for our lives. The Bible is profitable for bringing us such doctrine, that is, teaching. The scriptures teach us about who God is and how to walk with Him properly.

At times, people need to know that they are misunderstanding the Lord or are drifting off of His path for their lives. Well, the Bible is also profitable for reproof, that is, telling us when we are thinking or behaving wrongly.

Whenever we are off course concerning God, we not only need a word of reproof, but we also need to know how to get back on track spiritually. The scriptures are profitable for this as well. They can give us a word of correction, helping us to adjust our reasoning or conduct to God's ways.

In addition to teaching, reproving, and correcting, God's word is also able to train us in righteousness. This capacity of the word is so important, since once we are back on God's path, we need to be able to make progress on it. The scriptures are able to bring us along in the righteous ways of God.

These abilities of the word of God are some of the resources that He uses to shape and equip our lives to serve Him. Additionally, they are truths that we are to pass on to others in times of personal ministry and counseling.

Equipped for Every Good Work

To the extent that we receive the scriptures for teaching, reproof, correction, and training, our lives are made more complete in spiritual development and more equipped for godly service. In fact, this process of having God's word at work in our lives is potentially so effective that we can be *"thoroughly equipped for every good work."*

This equipping procedure through the word of God does not merely promise that we can be "partially" equipped for "some" good works. The pledge from the Lord is far more radical than that. It gives us the assurance of being fully prepared for any spiritual task that God desires us to undertake. The scriptures outfit us completely to participate in the good work of ministry. This would include ministering to others in prayer, in discipleship, in hospitality, in teaching - - in whatever the Lord calls us to do, including counseling.

Working in the Word

One aspect of letting the word of God do its equipping work in us is to be those who are diligently working in the word. 2 Timothy 2:15 addresses this subject:

> *"Be diligent to present yourself approved to God, a workman who does not need to be ashamed, handling accurately the word of truth"* (NASB).

129

Whoever desires to be used of God to counsel His way will want to persistently get into the scriptures. As the King James Version reads: *"Study to show yourself approved unto God."* Our use of the Bible in any area of life, including counseling, should have God's approval. Therefore, it is imperative that we earnestly study His word, so that we will handle it accurately, learning to let it say what the Spirit of God intends and not what the flesh of man prefers.

There is a desperate need in the body of Christ for biblical laborers, those who want to be precise in their use of God's word. Many people seeking counseling are left in bondage or brokenness or confusion, because the ones who are counseling them have not been diligent in studying the word of God. Others searching for help are sent off with false hopes or self-centered priorities or humanistic explanations, because the counselor was irresponsible with the scriptures.

God calls His servants to be workers in the word, taking time to read it, meditate on it, pray about its meaning, and consider its implications. This would include asking the Lord to clarify what He is saying in one passage by what He has stated in another passage, letting scripture explain scripture. Such care with the word of truth will be used of God to set people free and make them whole. May the Lord stir in us a diligence for the

Word of God, if we want to be equipped for the ministry of counseling.

Protection from "Cutting Off Ears"

One of the more important benefits that derives from being equipped by the scriptures is that we become increasingly protected from using the word in an irresponsible or destructive manner. Those who are somewhat skeptical regarding "one another counseling" are concerned that some would-be counselors will be using their spiritual swords, their Bibles, carelessly. They fear that the result could be similar to Peter's impulsive and misguided use of his sword in the garden of Gethsemane. In that instance, the high priest's servant had his ear inappropriately cut off.

That frightening scenario is certainly a possibility. In fact, many of us have probably done something like that, as we attempted to help another believer. It is most likely true that virtually everyone who has ever been willing to minister to others has "cut off a few ears" as they began to serve the Lord. When I started out as a pastor in the late 1960's, I know that I inadvertently sliced off a few ears through my careless use of the scriptures.

Now, I am not in favor of Christians indiscriminately hacking away at other Christians under the guise of carrying out their one another ministry. Such reckless and unloving behavior is wrong and unacceptable. However, we cannot leave the counseling ministry to a few experts (who are often worldly-trained at that) hoping to ensure that none of the rest of us cut anyone's ears off. Even those so-called experts undoubtedly chopped off a few ears when they started out. Anyway, such an unbiblical and overly protective approach would prohibit the counseling ministry from developing among all of God's people as He intends.

God's Protective Guidelines

Furthermore, God has His built-in spiritual guidelines that are designed to diminish this potential danger in personal ministry and discipling. We will give more thorough attention to such issues later on, but mentioning a few now would be profitable.

Matthew 7:3-5 offers considerable assistance in this area:

> *"And why do you look at the speck in your brother's eye, but do not consider the plank in your own eye? Or how can you say to your brother, 'Let me remove the speck from your eye'; and look, a plank is in your own eye? Hypocrite! First remove the plank from your own eye, and then you will see clearly to remove the speck from your brother's eye."*

If we are willing to allow the Lord to deal with problems and sins in our own lives, we then will be more likely to *"see clearly to remove the speck from* (our) *brother's eye."*

James 1:19-21 supplies further significant protection against haphazard "chopping away at others," and then trying to call it ministry:

> *"So then, my beloved brethren, let every man be swift to hear, slow to speak, slow to wrath; for the wrath of man does not produce the righteousness of God. Therefore lay aside all filthiness and overflow of wickedness, and receive with meekness the implanted word, which is able to save your souls."*

These patterns of living construct a wonderful safeguard for spiritual ministry. Consider them: eager to listen, careful with words, slow to anger, purged of ungodliness, humble receivers of God's word. Any child of God, who will let the Lord fashion his service more and more into the walk described in these verses, will increasingly become a counselor of spiritual healing, instead of fleshly hacking.

Growing in Knowing the Lord

Another way to avoid offering inappropriate personal ministry is to grow in knowing the Lord. Nothing will equip us to counsel God's way more than getting to know the

Lord better. 2 Peter 3:18 speaks of this profound privilege of developing a maturing relationship with the Savior:

> *"But grow in the grace and knowledge of
> our Lord and Savior Jesus Christ."*

God wants His children to grow. He
wants us to go from milk to meat, from spiritual babes to spiritual adults, from being served
to serving. Well, here is the heart of what
growing is all about: growing in the grace and
the knowledge of the Lord. Oh, how this will
maximize one's counseling ministry!

Growing in God's Grace

The grace of the Lord is what He supplies
to all who humbly look to Him. This includes
forgiveness and everlasting life, but it goes far
beyond these priceless blessings. God's grace
includes daily help and nurture and strength.
His grace makes transformation, fruitfulness,
and spiritual victory possible. All of this
and more is freely offered to all who do not
deserve it, cannot earn it, and are unable to
produce it on their own. To grow in this
grace and live by it marvelously prepares us
to counsel others, since only God's grace is
sufficient to meet their deepest needs.

(**Note**: A variety of audio and video
albums on "**Growing in the Grace of God**" are
available for further study on this subject. See

the Living in Christ Ministries Resources at the back of this book.)

A Developing Acquaintanceship with God

As we grow in the grace of God, we develop an increasing acquaintanceship with Him. It clearly follows that the more we understand His grace, the more we will understand the very heart of our Lord, and the more His majesty will impact our lives. The greatest need all of us have is to know the Lord better.

We can easily comprehend what a growing relationship with God would do to one's counseling ministry. The Lord Jesus is the Wonderful Counselor. He wants to use us as His instruments in offering His counsel. To the extent that we know Him, our counsel will truly be His counsel expressed through our lives. This is the goal for equipping in counseling ministry.

Conclusion

Many Christians often wonder about how they can be **equipped for any ministry** in general, or even counseling in particular. Well, God has not overlooked this important issue. He has built it into the very life of the church, the body of Christ. Consequently, man's educational programs in psychological theory will not be needed. In fact, if we already have them, the word of God indicates the need to lay these earthly philosophies aside.

God Himself will prepare and outfit our lives for service as we properly relate to Him, to His word, to His appointed leadership, and to one another. Then, as we exercise the gifts He has given to us and walk in His protective guidelines, we will develop in effectiveness and fruitfulness. In it all, we will grow in knowing Him, being transformed to serve, and counsel, as He did.

"Beloved, do not think it strange concerning the fiery trial which is to try you, as though some strange thing happened to you." — 1 Peter 4:12

Chapter 10
Uital Issues for Most Counseling Situations

The two previous chapters contained some of the Lord's provisions for equipping His people to counsel one another. **Vital biblical issues** will now be considered for further preparation in personal ministry. These strategic Bible truths come from two arenas of my own pilgrimage, as a disciple of the Lord Jesus Christ and as a pastor among His flock.

First, these passages from the word of God are some of those which have counseled my own heart and life most deeply during the past thirty-three years of walking with Christ. Second, these same portions of scripture have been used of the Lord profoundly over the last thirty years of pastoral counseling ministry with hungry and hurting lives.

I commend these truths to each reader both for personal use and for sharing with others. However, they will no doubt be of the greatest use with others if they are first personally received and followed. In other words, let's ask the Lord to first counsel us through these life-shaping realities. Then we will be more equipped to impart them to others.

A Lesson from Perplexity

More than twenty years ago, God sent my way a number of counseling opportunities that left me perplexed. Session after session, as I listened to struggling believers pour out their hearts, no specific biblical insight came to mind in regard to their dilemmas. However, something very significant had occurred during the first of this series of baffling encounters.

Just before suggesting that I had nothing specific to offer, I began to communicate some of the truths we will consider. That person went away greatly encouraged and strengthened, even though I was unable to present any specific "when this occurs, the Bible says to do this" type of counsel.

I followed this same pattern in the midst of each perplexing situation. To my amazement, every one of these ten or twelve bewildered saints left much comforted and deeply touched by the Lord. Since then, I have passed on these same truths to thousands of people. Time and time again, God has supplied His unique encouragement through these portions of His word, which unfold the following vital issues.

Trials, Difficulties, and Impossibilities

Trials, difficulties, and impossibilities are the very experiences which most often provoke a quest for counseling. The prevailing thoughts in the minds of those struggling through uncomfortable times are often inaccurate, as well as painful. Typically, their thinking includes such fallacies as: "This difficulty is so strange" and "This is pointless" and "There is no way out of this." Well, let's see what our Wonderful Counselor has to say about this subject in His word.

The Commonplace Nature of Trials

1 Peter 4:12 addresses this area:

"Beloved, do not think it strange concerning the fiery trial which is to try you, as though some strange thing happened to you."

It is not unusual for a counseling situation to begin with a statement similar to this: "The strangest thing has happened to me." Then, a description of the ordeal follows, accompanied by the deep sense of shock and surprise at what is being experienced. This type of thinking is certainly understandable. Nevertheless, we are really not to be surprised when trials occur. It is not a strange thing, when a fiery ordeal comes upon us. We are told here that the unpleasant adventure is for our spiritual testing.

There is a type of trial that is inappropriate and should diminish in our lives, as we grow in the Lord. 1 Peter 4:15 tells us of this kind:

> *"But let none of you suffer as a murderer, a thief, an evildoer, or as a busybody in other people's matters."*

Such suffering results from something we are doing wrong, indulging in fleshly living and disobeying the Lord. If we are suffering that way, God desires that we repent of it and look to Him to forgive us and lead us again in His path. This is not the type of suffering we are considering at this time. Rather, we are examining the more perplexing variety, that is, suffering that is related to walking in paths of godliness.

The Benefits of Trials

1 Peter 1:6-7 speaks of godly suffering and indicates some of the spiritual benefits that can result:

> *"In this you greatly rejoice, though now for a little while, if need be, you have been*

grieved by various trials, that the genuine-
ness of your faith, being much more pre-
cious than gold that perishes, though it
is tested by fire, may be found to praise,
honor, and glory at the revelation of Jesus
Christ."

Although we have great cause for rejoicing in the Christian life, we can also face considerable grief as a consequence of the assort-
ed trials that come our way. Yet, such grief
is certainly worth the discomfort, because of
the spiritual dividends that it may produce.
Through the challenging situations of life, our
faith can be demonstrated as genuine. When
difficulties arise, they provide an opportunity
to trust in the Lord. Observers can see that
our claim to faith in God is real, not merely
religious words. We also are thereby given a
chance to see the reality of our own dependency upon the Lord.

Additionally, our faith is refined unto
greater purity and reality. In this scripture, God
likens faith unto gold, which goes through a
refining process. Gold ore is intensely heated,
so that the worthless dross might be separated
from that which is precious. Similarly, God
takes us through circumstantial fires, that true
faith in Him might be separated from dependence upon ourselves or others. Ultimately,
all of this process climaxes at the return of the
Lord Jesus, when He gets all of the honor and

glory for what He did in each situation, as we trusted in Him.

James 1:2-4 gives more divine insight on this theme of godly suffering and the benefits that can be derived from them:

"My brethren, count it all joy when you fall into various trials, knowing that the testing of your faith produces patience. But let patience have its perfect work, that you may be perfect and complete, lacking nothing."

When trials come our way, we are to consider it a reason for joy. This does not mean that we are to enjoy suffering. Rather, we are to consider our trials, all of them, as a matter for joy. Such a perspective is an act of faith. The difficulties of life are not enjoyable in themselves. Nevertheless, by faith, we see what God can do with them, and it stirs rejoicing in our hearts.

Notice, it does not say **if** they come, but **when** they come. Here we have another indication that trials are a normal part of Christian experience. Also notice, it refers to *"various trials,"* indicating there is a range of variety that should not surprise us. Now and then, they not only come one right after another, they seem to all come at once. During these periods, we need to know something that is revealed here. *"Knowing that the testing of your faith produces patience."* When times are tough, God wants us to fully rely upon this truth: He can use trials to produce patience in us. If we trust in the Lord in the midst of stretching adversities, He brings spiritual stamina, godly steadfastness, and Christ-like endurance into our character. This is one way that God completes and perfects our lives experientially.

We need to **know** that the testing of our faith produces endurance. Those seeking counsel and those giving counsel need to know this. The general tendency of a person in a trial is to only seek relief. The typical counsel given to the one who is in a trial is aimed only at getting out of that plight. God can certainly give relief and bring deliverance. However, we do not want to overlook any bigger work of transformation that He may desire to do.

Ordinarily, it is through difficulties that we grow the most. God wants us to grow to be mature and complete, that is, whole in Christ. The wholeness of life that we need is found in Christ. Colossians 2:10a says, *"you are complete in Him"* (we will study this glorious issue in Section Four on "Foundational Truths"). In trials, our flesh is circumcised, while our faith is exercised. In times of difficulty, our human resources are shown as inadequate. Consequently, we must depend upon that which only the Lord can supply. We must draw upon the wholeness that is already ours in Christ.

Psychological Counseling and Trials

This brings up another matter of concern regarding the use of psychological theory in counseling, particularly in so-called Christian counseling. Psychological theory appeals to and builds hope in the flesh, the natural resources of humanity. God, on the other hand, wants to crucify the flesh, showing its spiritual bankruptcy. Psychological theory offers to the flesh an endless supply of ideas and approaches through which man might manage or cope without the necessity of leaning wholly upon the Lord.

In the midst of great testings, God brings a person to another encounter with the cross of discipleship. This lays before an individual the heavenly option of saying no to self and death to self (see Luke 9:23). Hereby, they will be prepared to exercise that life-giving choice to press on to follow Christ, finding all that is needed in Him. The interjection of psychological theory at this point proposes the possibility of a detour around the cross, keeping the self-life intact to try manipulating its way through another challenging moment. May the Lord alert us to these psychological diversions, both in the counsel that we seek, as well as the counsel that we give.

Growing in Faith through Impossibilities

Whether we indulge in carnal psychological diversions or press after the Lord, God at times places radical impossibilities in our path to grow our trust in Him. Even the godly Apostle Paul was not immune to such experiences, as 2 Corinthians 1:8-10 reveals:

"For we do not want you to be unaware, brethren, of our affliction which came to us in Asia, that we were burdened excessively, beyond our strength, so that we despaired even of life; indeed, we had the sentence of death within ourselves in order that we should not trust in ourselves, but in God who raises the dead; who delivered us from so great a peril of death, and will deliver us, He on whom we have set our hope. And He will yet deliver us" (NASB).

Notice the terms that indicate the intolerable dimensions of this adversity: *"our affliction . . . burdened excessively . . . beyond our strength . . . despaired even of life . . . the sentence of death within ourselves."*

Affliction speaks of troubles or pressures. Excessive burden shows that the load was too much to bear. Beyond strength tells of having spent all of the energy that was available. Despairing of life suggests that all hope was gone. Internal sentence of death implies a deep depression. This trial had gone beyond extreme difficulty into the realm of total impossibility.

Don't forget who was writing this testimony: the Apostle Paul. He was undoubtedly the most faithful and fruitful leader in the first century church. Yet, he and his team underwent astounding impossibilities. Certainly, if Paul had to face such times, we will as well. We are not told exactly what happened to him. Most likely, the Lord purposefully kept the details hidden, so that we would all the more apply these truths to our own impossibilities.

Whenever a child of God is walking in the will of God and serving Him faithfully, impossible trials can seem exceedingly pointless. In verse 9, the simple phrase *"in order that"* reveals that God had some determined purpose for this impossibility. These three words assure us that our seemingly futile trials can head toward a valuable conclusion.

"In order that we should not trust in ourselves, but in God who raises the dead." We all know that it is desirable to grow in our trust toward God. However, this often requires that we learn more deeply not to trust in ourselves. Therefore, the Lord puts us into extreme situations that purge us of self-dependence, so that we will more quickly and more fully put our trust in Him alone. As we trust in the God who raises the dead, He raises us out of our deadening circumstance, just as He

will raise us later from the grave. Encouraged to set our hope on Him daily, we anticipate His on-going delivering work on our behalf.

These faith-developing words lead to another category of vital issues that can be exceedingly fruitful in most counseling encounters.

Hope, Encouragement, and Assurance

When in trials, difficulties, and impossibilities, it is so important to find hope, encouragement, and assurance. However, these virtues must be those which come from God Himself, not merely derived from human opinions and cultural traditions. The word of God abounds with such blessings, as exemplified by 1 Corinthians 10:13:

> *"No temptation has overtaken you except such as is common to man; but God is faithful, who will not allow you to be tempted beyond what you are able, but with the temptation will also make the way of escape, that you may be able to bear it."*

The temptations and trials that we encounter are not unique. Much anguish arises from entertaining the thought that no one has ever gotten into a predicament quite as bizarre or foolish as our own. Yet, *"No temptation has overtaken you except such as is common to man."* Others have been in, and are probably now in, similar situations.

God's Faithfulness

Here is our hope during testings and trials: *"God is faithful."* We can rely upon Him. He is dependable. We can trust Him to not allow any difficulty to come upon us that would be too much for us to bear. This truth may stretch our credulity at times. Nevertheless, God knows perfectly well that as we depend on Him we are enabled to face faith-enlarging challenges.

In addition to supervising the dimensions of our trials, the Lord *"will also make the way of escape."* He provides the appropriate avenue to eventually leave the impossibilities behind. Generally, it appears that God's way of escape is to go through them to the end, as indicated by the phrase, *"that you may be able to bear* (endure) *it."*

We could liken the testings of life to a tunnel. The way out is to go through to the designed end. We would often prefer that there would be a manhole or escape hatch right over our head, through which the Lord might snatch us out of the fiery ordeal. Praise be to God, sometimes an instantaneous release is available. Still, the general route of deliverance from trials is to find sustaining grace from the Lord to endure until He determines that all pertinent spiritual matters have been fully accomplished. In any case, God's faithfulness is our source of encouragement throughout this entire process.

After the Suffering

1 Peter 5:10 presents another great word of hope and encouragement. It concerns what can follow a period of distress.

> *"And after you have suffered for a little while, the God of all grace, who called you to His eternal glory in Christ will Himself, perfect, confirm, strengthen and establish you"* (NASB).

Those who know the Lord Jesus Christ have been invited to share in the everlasting glories of God. Between now, here on earth, and later, there in heaven, God has things that He wants to do in our lives. He wants to *"perfect, confirm, strengthen and establish"* us in the faith. In order to prepare our lives for the work He desires to do in us, suffering is allowed to come our way at times. When it comes, it may seem to linger endlessly. Yet in the perspective of eternity, the time is actually brief.

Notice, however, that the One who is at work on us and in us is *"the God of all grace."* He has gracious reasons for permitting the suffering. He offers His sustaining grace to see us through the difficulty. He graciously concludes the season of adversity when He deems it appropriate. He reshapes our character by His transforming grace. Whatever measure or type of grace is needed, *"the God of all grace"* can abundantly provide it.

After the necessary suffering has run its full course, God Himself concludes the entire process by imparting those effects that only He can produce. He perfects us, making us more mature spiritually. He confirms us, granting us more assurance in our Christian walk. He strengthens us, leaving us more fortified by the resources of Christ. He establishes us, giving us a more settled relationship with Him.

This is a vital word of hope to those who are struggling. They may be right on the verge of having the Lord Himself bring forth new measures of these godly consequences in their lives.

Our God with Us

God previously had proclaimed related words of hope for His people in Isaiah 41:10:

> *"Fear not, for I am with you; be not dismayed, for I am your God. I will strengthen you, yes, I will help you, I will uphold you with My righteous right hand."*

During trials, difficulties, and impossibilities, panic and anxiety can attack relentlessly. Yet, there is a sufficient reality that brings us comfort and assurance. We do not have to face the struggle alone. Our God is with us. Furthermore, He gives a three-fold promise to undertake on our behalf in the very ways in which we are so needy. He **will strengthen us**, when we are weak. He **will help us**, when we are inadequate. He **will uphold us**, when we are about to collapse.

These truths are related to another vital issue that pertains to most counseling situations, that is, the resources upon which we must ultimately rely.

God's Resources, Not Ours

As those receiving counsel and giving counsel, we need to increasingly learn to rely on God's resources, not ours. This is very clearly stated in 2 Corinthians 3:5:

> *"Not that we are sufficient of ourselves to think of anything as being from ourselves, but our sufficiency is from God."*

Man is not the source of what man needs. Even we who are forgiven by the Lord and have been given new life in Christ are not *"sufficient of ourselves to think of anything as being from ourselves."* Apart from the Lord living in us and working through us, we cannot adequately produce what life demands or what God desires.

This is both humbling and liberating. It is humbling to realize that we do not innately have within us what is essential for true living. Yet, it is liberating to know that God does not expect us to produce the necessary elements of an acceptable life before Him.

(**Note:** A six-hour audio tape album on "**God's Sufficiency for Godly Living**" is available for further study on this subject. See the Living in Christ Ministries Resources at the back of this book.)

Sufficiency in General

Many saints seeking counseling for a variety of reasons commonly struggle to face their situations by their own sufficiency. Consequently, although their detailed circumstances may vary greatly, they all agonize over the same sense of personal inadequacy. What a blessing God has for each of them, as they are directed away from their own limited resources to the infinite resources of Almighty God.

The futile battle to find adequacy within self to deal with a present problem can become a far greater burden than the problem itself. Whether someone is anguishing over a lack of insight, peace, strength, resolve, love, self-control, or whatever, the basic need is the same. All of these capacities must come from

God, not from ourselves. Everyone must find their source of sufficiency in the Lord alone.

It was in the late 1960's and early 70's that the Lord began to introduce me to this vital issue of relying on His resources, instead of my own. This truth was to become one of those personal, priceless, life-changing realities of the word of God. I was trying so hard in those years to be "Mr. All-Christian," to be "Mr. Everything-Pastor." The demands of pastoring were far more than I had ever imagined. Yet, I wanted to serve and please the Lord. He had done so much for me. The least that I could do was to be adequate and effective for Him. This perspective may have indicated well-intended devotion toward God. However, it also demonstrated a lack of awareness concerning the suitable source of sufficiency for growth and service.

I was getting very tired and quite discouraged. Maybe I did not have what it took to walk in fruitfulness and faithfulness. This glorious truth that God did not expect me to produce an effective Christian life on my own was living water to a dry and weary soul. *"Not that we are sufficient of ourselves to think of anything as being from ourselves."* Furthermore, I was exhilarated and encouraged to discover God's sufficiency was available as I depended upon Him. *"But our sufficiency is from God."*

We do not have to manufacture righteousness, peace, hope, joy, wisdom, victory, and strength. Such spiritual necessities do not come from us. Nonetheless, they can flow unceasingly to us from our Lord God. It is a matter of God's resources, not ours. This vital issue is one we want to live by and share in any counseling situation.

Sufficiency of Wisdom and Direction

In the general area of adequacy for living, wisdom is one particular attribute that is so often needed, but so often lacking in our own resources. In Proverbs 3:5-6, the Lord offers His remedy for this predicament:

> *"Trust in the LORD with all your heart, and lean not on your own understanding; in all your ways acknowledge Him, and He shall direct your paths."*

Finding the proper path through the maze of life's circumstances regularly leaves people in a virtual paralysis of bewilderment and indecision. In many situations what is really appropriate is not mountains of advice from well-meaning counselors, who feel that they must provide the ultimate resolution for every dilemma on earth. Rather, the true need is to assist people in learning how to allow the Lord to guide their path, using His matchless understanding and wisdom.

Experiencing God's guidance involves, first of all, putting all of our hope and expectations upon Him. *"Trust in the LORD with all your heart."* Additionally, we are to refuse to count upon our own best analysis of the situation. *"Lean not on your own understanding."* Finally, we acknowledge the Lord as the One who can handle every aspect of the difficulty that we are facing. *"In all your ways acknowledge Him."* In this confession, we are looking to Jesus to be to us the Wonderful Counselor that He is declared to be in the scriptures. Praying and reading the word of God would certainly be appropriate ways to demonstrate that we are hoping in the Lord and not in ourselves. The instrument of godly human counsel would not be ruled out, as long as our hearts are set upon the Lord and want His Spirit to convict or direct.

Then, the wonderful consequence of this spiritual disposition before God is that we can rest in His promise to guide us. *"And He shall direct your paths."* What a bedrock certainty this affords to the trusting soul! We may not be able to direct a troubled individual along the precise path that he should follow. However, we can be used of God in a much more profound manner. We can help that bewildered person to go on his way with an inner confidence that the Lord will faithfully and wisely direct his path through his impossibility, and even through the ones that may yet lie ahead.

In the quest for sufficiency of wisdom and direction, it is a matter of God's resources, not ours.

Sufficiency of Strength

Strength is another regularly needed attribute for living. Here again, human resources consistently prove to be insufficient. Isaiah 40:29-31 reveals the only source of strength that will prove adequate for the demands of living. Also, this passage shows who qualifies for this strength, as well as how to access it.

> *"He gives power to the weak, and to those who have no might He increases strength. Even the youths shall faint and be weary, and the young men shall utterly fall, but those who wait on the LORD shall renew their strength; they shall mount up with wings like eagles, they shall run and not be weary, they shall walk and not faint."*

Many of those seeking counsel are motivated by a sense of personal weakness and weariness. The issues they face are draining their limited capacities. We can point them to the inexhaustible source of the strength they need. The Lord Himself is the supplier. *"He gives power . . . He increases strength."* Those who qualify as recipients of this might that comes from God are those who will humbly admit that they are in need. *"He gives power to the **weak** . . . to those who have **no might**."*

Too many struggling men and women fail to find the strength they are desperately searching for, because they will not humbly face their own weakness before God.

Whenever we acknowledge our lack of power and admit that God must be our source, waiting upon the Lord becomes the means of access to this heavenly might. *"Those who **wait** on the LORD shall renew their strength."* Waiting upon the Lord encompasses more than merely allowing time to pass. It applies as much to resting in a rocking chair as it does to racing to beat a deadline. It is not a physical action or inaction. Rather, it is a spiritual attitude. There is a time to sit and a time to run, a time to tarry and a time to proceed. However, in every condition, we must learn to wait on the Lord.

Waiting upon the Lord involves putting our hope in God, placing our expectations upon Him and counting on Him to provide what is needed. Such exercising of our faith allows us to walk in His unfailing promises to supply all necessary sustaining power.

> *"Those who wait on the LORD **shall** renew their strength; they **shall** mount up with wings like eagles, they **shall** run and not be weary, they **shall** walk and not faint."*

Again, in the arena of finding sufficiency of strength, it is a matter of God's resources, not ours.

Sufficiency for Victory

Impending defeat from overwhelming circumstances is another common factor in life that reveals the inadequacy of mere human resources. Sometimes the difficulty is like one foreboding giant, obstructing the path. At other times, the adversity is like being surrounded by multiple armies, leaving no way out. Such dilemmas drive many people to seek relief through counseling. God's word has a vital insight for us when we are in these situations, or for us to give to others who may be similarly embattled.

Confronted by a Giant

1 Samuel 17:45-47 speaks of the threatening giants that confront us at times. Here David speaks to Goliath, who signified almost certain defeat for the people of God.

"Then David said to the Philistine, 'You come to me with a sword, with a spear, and with a javelin. But I come to you in the name of the LORD of hosts, the God of the armies of Israel, whom you have defied. This day the LORD will deliver you into my hand, and I will strike you and take your head from you. And this day I will give the carcasses of the camp of the Philistines to the birds of the air and the wild beasts of the earth, that all the earth

*may know that there is a God in Israel.
Then all this assembly shall know that the
LORD does not save with sword and spear;
for the battle is the Lord's, and He will give
you into our hands'."*

Goliath was a formidable foe. David could
not match him in size or in human weaponry.
However, David came against him *"in the
name of the Lord,"* that is, depending upon
God and His resources. *"This day the LORD
will deliver you into my hand."* David's ultimate confidence was *"the battle is the Lord's."*

With that underlying absolute as his hope,
David ran expectantly toward the giant, having
prepared his familiar sling (verses 48-49).

*"And it was so, when the Philistine arose
and came and drew near to meet David,
that David hastened and ran toward the
army to meet the Philistine. Then David
put his hand in his bag and took out a
stone; and he slung it and struck the
Philistine in his forehead, so that the stone
sank into his forehead, and he fell on his
face to the earth."*

David utilized what God had previously
taught him to use, and the Lord gave him victory over the giant.

Surrounded by Multiple Armies

In 2 Chronicles 20:1, we find another perspective on this same truth. However, the specific circumstances are significantly different. Here, God's man is surrounded by multiple armies, instead of facing a formidable giant.

> *"It happened after this that the people of Moab with the people of Ammon, and others with them besides the Ammonites, came to battle against Jehoshaphat."*

Furthermore, unlike David, who ran boldly against his foe with a clear plan in his mind, Jehoshaphat was totally overwhelmed and completely perplexed (verse 12).

> *"O our God, will You not judge them? For we have no power against this great multitude that is coming against us; nor do we know what to do, but our eyes are upon You."*

Jehoshaphat felt utterly inadequate, and he had no plan of action. Yet, he began to appeal to the Lord. Then, God offered him the same basic hope that David stood upon many years earlier (verses 14-15).

> *"Then the Spirit of the LORD came upon Jahaziel the son of Zechariah . . . and he said, 'Listen, all you of Judah and you inhabitants of Jerusalem, and you, King Jehoshaphat! Thus says the LORD to you: Do not be afraid nor dismayed because of*

*this great multitude, for the battle is not
yours, but God's'."*

The fundamental truth would again be **"the
battle is the Lord's, not ours."** This reality would
now be demonstrated in an entirely new manner. Jehoshaphat would not even have to deal
directly with his impossible circumstances. God
was going to intervene more directly than He
had with David (verse 17).

*"You will not need to fight in this battle.
Position yourselves, stand still and see the
salvation of the LORD, who is with you, O
Judah and Jerusalem! Do not fear or be
dismayed; tomorrow go out against them,
for the LORD is with you."*

This remarkable promise stirred the people to give worship and praise unto the Lord.
As they poured their adoration upon God, He
confounded the enemy to destroy one another
(verse 20).

*"Now when they began to sing and to
praise, the LORD set ambushes against the
people of Ammon, Moab, and Mount Seir,
who had come against Judah; and they
were defeated. For the people of Ammon
and Moab stood up against the inhabitants of Mount Seir to utterly kill and
destroy them. And when they had made
an end of the inhabitants of Seir, they
helped to destroy one another."*

The earthly circumstances that David and Jehoshaphat faced seemed so different on the surface. David was confronted by a single giant, whereas Jehoshaphat was encompassed by an alliance of three nations. David knew exactly what he should do and took aggressive action to accomplish it. Conversely, Jehoshaphat had no certainty of direction and passively drew back from the conflict.

The similarities between the two episodes are far more profound than the differences, however. Ultimately, both men found sufficient resources for victory. This was because they both depended upon what God could accomplish, not upon what they could achieve. David went into action believing that *"the battle is the Lord's."* Jehoshaphat expectantly stood still believing the prophetic word through Jahaziel that *"the battle is not yours, but God's."*

How to find sufficiency for victory is a vital issue when we face impossible circumstances, or are ministering to others who are facing the same. Whether confronted by a giant of a circumstance or surrounded by multiple armies of circumstances, we all need to see that *"the battle is the Lord's."* We do not have within us the sufficiency to produce victory on our own. Neither do we attempt to become, or to avoid becoming, an aggressive David or a passive Jehoshaphat.

When circumstances are overwhelming

and defeat appears certain, victory depends upon God's resources, not ours.

Looking to the Lord

Another way to view all of these vital issues is to always look to the Lord. Hebrews 12:1-2 speaks of this important matter in the imagery of running the race of life:

> *". . . let us run with endurance the race that is set before us, looking unto Jesus, the author and perfecter of our faith . . . ."*

Living the Christian life is like running a race. Yes, it contains countless blessings, but they can be periodically eclipsed by the challenges. The race can become arduous and relentless. It can sometimes appear to be a marathon and a steeplechase combined, with intermittent one hundred meter dashes. Endurance is definitely required.

Many individuals seek counsel because their stamina is fading. Their temptation is to focus in any direction but the one that will supply endurance. Producing the necessary perseverance on our own generally seems like the most reasonable option. Typically, friends, colleagues, and professional Christian therapists will urge us to draw upon our own resources. They may even offer well-meaning exhortations of, "You've got it in you; just hang in there," or "Dig down deep inside, and you will find all that you need." Clearly, from the perspective of the scriptures, this is not counseling God's way.

Jesus Authoring Our Faith

The word of God emphasizes that *"the just shall live by faith"* (Romans 1:17). The Christian life from beginning to end develops from trusting in the Lord. Our passage in Hebrews 12 describes Jesus as the author of faith. When we began the life of faith, Jesus authored that faith in our lives. He did this by presenting Himself to us as the One who can be trusted for salvation. Through some presentation of the gospel, He offered Himself as Lord and Savior. In His person we saw that the Lord God had come as a man. In His death we saw a payment for our sins. In Him we saw new life available to us. All the while, the Holy Spirit convicted us of the reality of His claims, as well as of our need to have forgiveness and new life. So, we put our trust in this One who was worthy to be trusted, and faith was authored in us.

Jesus Perfecting Our Faith

Similarly, if our faith is to grow and develop, Jesus must also be the perfecter of our faith. He utilizes the same methodology as He did in authoring faith in us. He reveals Himself to us through His word, unfolding His matchless character and limitless resources and effective works on our behalf. Then, He works appropriately in us in accordance with what He has disclosed in His word. In all of this, the Lord demonstrates Himself as trust-worthy, so we progressively exercise more and more trust in Him. Throughout this process, Jesus is perfecting faith in the lives of those who are looking to Him, focusing their atten-tions and expectations upon Him. One of the results is that we find in and from Him the endurance that the race of life demands.

The only way that the people of God can run with endurance the race that is set before them is by looking to Jesus, the author and perfecter of faith.

Psychological Counseling and Looking to Jesus

One of the great failures of modern day Christian counseling, in its attempt to integrate psychological humanistic theory with biblical spiritual truth, is that it typically produces counseling that does not focus upon the Lord. Rather, it encourages people to become occu-pied with self and others and circumstances and the past. Then, their hope is to be found in endless earthbound speculations that pur-port to offer life's remedies concerning all of these matters. Such counsel does not develop faith in the Lord, nor does it bring spiritual stamina from the Lord.

Conclusion

In being equipped to counsel God's way, **vital issues** like the ones we have been considering can prove to be invaluable. We want to be ready to impart to others the Lord's truth about "**Trials, Difficulties**, and **Impossibilities**," "**Hope, Encouragement**, and **Assurance**," "**God's Resources, Not Ours**" and "**Looking to the Lord**."

This list is certainly not exhaustive regarding what is needful in counseling others. Yet, it demonstrates how much God can do with even a few proclamations of His incomparable light and truth. I encourage you to read them, study them, pray over them, and meditate on them. Also, ask God to enable you to walk in them. Then, allow the Lord to use you to share them at appropriate times with others. You may be amazed at how broadly applicable they are, and yet how deeply they speak to people's lives and needs.

In addition, ask our Wonderful Counselor to increasingly unfold for you a **growing list of such vital issues**. Then, as He uses those truths to shape your life, be ready in counseling opportunities to pass them on to others. This is one of the fundamental ways that God equips us to be more fruitful and effective in personal ministry to others.

Keep in mind that the great way to be prepared to counsel others is to have God consistently counseling us. If we look to God to counsel us, He will surely use us to extend His counsel to others. Sometimes, we can circumvent this process. We hear something from the word, and we can't wait to give it to somebody else. While it is good to have that desire, let us first take that truth into our own lives, asking God to work it into our walk with Him. Then, we will be more properly equipped to share it with others.

"Be anxious for nothing, but in everything by prayer and supplication, with thanksgiving, let your requests be made known to God." — Philippians 4:6

Chapter 11
Guidelines for the Counseling Situation

Another realm of equipping that can be exceedingly helpful is **guidelines for the counseling situation**. As we should anticipate, the scriptures are rich with insights applicable to any type of counseling session. We can look into the word of God to find out what should be occurring when one person sits down with another, seeking to know the mind of the Lord on any given matter of life.

The biblical precepts and patterns that we will now consider are appropriate for **every variety of counseling situation**, whether formal or informal, whether planned or spontaneous, whether involving church staff or church leaders or any of the one another relationships among believers.

Proper Personal Walk

Guidelines from the Lord for personal ministry also involve the times that precede our sitting down to share with another person. Too easily we think of our counseling ministry as that moment when we may impart to someone a word of wisdom that will change his life. Well, by the grace of God at work in and through us that can happen. However, all ministry is to flow forth from a proper personal walk with the Lord. We cannot walk daily in any manner that our flesh may desire, and then fifteen minutes before we sit down with another person, remember that we need to prepare our hearts to be used of God.

Life and service in Christ involves a step-by-step, day-by-day walk with Him.

> *"I, therefore, the prisoner of the Lord, beseech you to have a **walk** worthy of the calling with which you were called, with all lowliness and gentleness, with longsuffering, bearing with one another in love . . . Therefore be followers of God as dear children. And **walk** in love, as Christ also has loved us . . . For you were once darkness, but now you are light in the Lord. **Walk** as children of light . . . See then that you **walk** circumspectly, not as fools but as wise . . ."* (Ephesians 4:1-2; 5:1-2, 8, 15).

Ideally, each step of every day is to be taken by following the Lord, walking in His unity, love, light, and wisdom. This is worthy of, or appropriate for, those who are called to carry the name of Jesus in this needy world. As we walk in this fashion more and more, we will be increasingly prepared for any counseling situation that may arise, whether anticipated or unforeseen.

Biblical Perspective on Counseling

In addition to a proper daily walk with God, a second guideline for personal ministry would be having a biblical perspective on counseling. Psalm 119:41 gives us the implications that we can consider regarding this guideline:

> *"Let Your mercies come also to me, O LORD - - Your salvation **according to Your word."***

In true biblical counseling, we are declaring the mercies and saving works of the Lord on behalf of man. In order to pass such realities on to others, we want God to reveal them to us. He does this *"according to His word,"* by means of, and in line with, His word. Consequently, we want to have a thoroughly biblical perspective on counseling.

Previously, we have seen that such a viewpoint includes the Lord as counselor, the path of discipleship, and the process of sanctification. Furthermore, we saw that the Lord brings His discipling and sanctifying counsel to us through His word, by the work of the Holy Spirit, into prayerful lives, amidst the one another relationships and ministries of His people living together in church-life. Consequently, these are the spiritual elements that should comprise our thinking and our convictions concerning the ministry of counseling.

This is a critical guideline for our own preparation before those face-to-face times arrive in personal ministry. Our commitment to these matters will be demonstrated by our ongoing walk in the word, by the Spirit, with much prayer, and within church-life.

Unfolding Aspects

The third guideline, which will receive most of our attention, encompasses various unfolding aspects of the counseling situation. This concept could also be examined as the "flow" of a counseling session. These terms, "unfolding aspects" and "flow," were prayerfully selected to avoid getting trapped in any tight counseling procedure that we compel people to undergo systematically.

We want to be very sensitive to the Spirit of the Lord in counseling one another. As with every area of Christian life and service, it must be *"not of the letter but of the Spirit; for the letter kills, but the Spirit gives life"* (2 Corinthians 3:6). God wants to use us as instruments of His life-giving counsel. He does not want us operating under a "letter of the law procedure" that deprives people of the life that only His Holy Spirit can impart.

As important as it is that we be committed to using the Bible in counseling, we must be similarly committed to the working of the Holy Spirit. The Spirit of God must be the One we depend upon to guide and work in both parties in the counseling situation, throughout the entire process. When we are counseling, or evaluating potential counseling resources, we need to look not only for biblical principles, but also for the role of the Holy Spirit.

Nonetheless, having stated all of this, there are certain biblical realities that are present in or applicable to virtually every counseling situation. The following is a list of such matters. They may not always appear, and they may appear in various sequences. Yet, they typically occur, and often in this order. Still, once again, anticipate that every situation is to be a dynamic work of God Himself.

Aspect #1: Praying about the Counseling Situation

Philippians 4:6 gives a significant picture of the importance of prayer in all of the

Christian life. It also contains some pertinent implications for the counseling situation.

> *"Be anxious for nothing, but in everything by prayer and supplication, with thanksgiving, let your requests be made known to God."*

Prayer is an essential part of counseling God's way. So often, the counseling situation is fraught with anxiety. The person seeking counsel is frequently very anxious, both with the problem, as well as with the prospect of inviting another person into dealing with the problem. Likewise, the person offering help is customarily concerned about whether he will prove to be helpful or not. Consequently, it is wise to saturate every counseling situation with prayer. This would include each person praying when approaching the session, praying together when beginning the session, and praying periodically in his heart throughout the session. In prayer, each participant can be looking to the Wonderful Counselor in all matters of apprehension.

Aspect #2: Listening to the Seekers' Concerns

Listening is also an important aspect of biblical counseling. Incidentally, if we really are listening attentively when someone pours out his heart to us, we will most likely be praying also. Ordinarily, what people are

going through is more than sufficient to provoke prayer in the life of anyone who is
attempting to offer godly assistance.

The fourth chapter of John provides a
divine picture of the place of listening in
biblical counseling. Therein, Jesus is sitting
at Jacob's well in Samaria, functioning as the
Wonderful Counselor, with a woman who had
profound spiritual needs. During their time
together, Jesus shared many glorious spiritual
realities with her. However, at times He
showed His love for her by listening to what
she had to say as well.

Jesus was a patient listener, as all four
Gospels clearly document. It is good to listen.
It is pleasing to the Lord to listen, because it
is part of the way He ministered to people.
Even today, our risen and ascended Lord still
gives loving attention to the cries of His people. Listening to what others have to say can
be one important way to demonstrate the caring love of God.

Furthermore, if the Son of God considered it appropriate to listen, how much more
should we. Unlike Jesus, we do not know
specifically what is in the heart of any given
individual. Proverbs 18:13 warns us of our
need to listen before answering:

> *"He who answers a matter before he hears
> it, it is folly and shame to him."*

As we prayerfully listen to those who are

seeking our help, the Lord can begin to give us the understanding to share His answers with them.

Aspect #3: Concerned about Initial Salvation

As we are proceeding into a counseling situation, we will want to pray and listen, listen and pray. We are listening to the matter being expressed by the one seeking our help. Yet, we are also listening for matters that may be of higher spiritual priority than what is on the other person's mind at the time. Initial salvation is God's highest priority for man. Consequently, in every counseling situation, we should always be concerned primarily about the seeker's salvation condition, if it is not apparent to us that they have already come to know the Lord.

Remember, when the Lord is allowed to be the counselor, He counsels with respect to the path of discipleship. As was noted earlier in Chapter Two, the great command of Jesus in Matthew 28:19, that would cover all of the life of His disciples thereafter, demands this perspective on counseling. *"Go therefore and make disciples of all the nations."* The Lord did not leave heaven above to die a cruel death on the cross here below in order to possibly produce more well-adjusted Christian citizens. He came to call out a band of disciples who would follow Him and begin to reach out to help others do the same.

This means that the Lord wants to use the person's problem to get them on the path of discipleship, if they do not yet know His saving grace. Therefore, the Lord desires that we be ever available as His instruments to share the gospel of salvation with any seeker who may need to hear it. Regardless of the stated reason why they came seeking our help, the greatest assistance that we can offer to them is to help them meet Jesus Christ as their own personal Lord and Savior.

Counseling Illustration

Some years ago, a mother came to see me. She was lovingly concerned about the engagement of her daughter to a young man in the church in which I was the Pastor. My dear friend and Assistant Pastor, John, and I sat down together with her one afternoon.

By the way, this counseling session brings up some important matters of wisdom for personal ministry. First, it is often beneficial to have a third party sit in on the counseling situation. That person can provide extra prayer support. Also, he may provide additional biblical insight along the way. Furthermore, this is a scripturally sound manner in which to train and develop spiritual counselors in the family of God. Finally, this third person can be a protecting presence, for instance, whenever a pastor or other brother is called upon to counsel a woman. Ideally, a godly sister in the Lord is the best instrument for personal ministry to a woman, although in certain cases it may not be possible to arrange or acceptable to the one seeking counsel.

So, returning to our story, John and I sat down with this dear concerned mother. With her permission, we began with a word of prayer, asking the Lord to guide us into His will in all that we would discuss. Then, she started to explain her distress. I was listening to her carefully and prayerfully, desiring to express God's love for her through my attentiveness. She had some valid concerns that pertained to both her daughter and the prospective son-in-law, which I readily acknowledged as I continued to listen.

Concurrently, while listening to what was on her heart, I was wondering about her salvation condition. The daughter and prospective son-in-law were both followers of the Lord Jesus. The mother had been attending our church services for only a brief period of time. I had no personal knowledge of her relationship with God. Thus, I was silently asking the Lord to give me some indication of where she stood with Him.

From the absence of any references to the Lord in her conversation, I was beginning to doubt that she knew Him. Then, I asked her if she had Christ in her life, in a way that she could turn to Him in this family crisis. By the look on her face and the perplexed comment she offered, I was quite certain that she was not yet on the path of discipleship. She needed to hear the call to come and follow Jesus. She needed to hear the gospel of salvation in Jesus Christ.

I asked if I could share some of the word of God, so that she would see how to have the Lord in her life for this present predicament, as well as for all of the other questions of life that were still ahead. She indicated that she would like me to do that. So I opened my Bible and began to read a number of initial salvation verses, without comment. I read verses like John 3:16; 14:6; Romans 3:23; 6:23; Ephesians 2:8-9; 1 John 5:11-13.

Eventually, as I continued reading various gospel verses, this openhearted mother dropped her head into her hands and began to sob. I commented that she seemed to have a deep sense of need for this saving grace that God's word was describing. She agreed immediately and earnestly. With my input on direction, she prayed, repenting of her sins, confessing her need of God's forgiveness, and putting her faith in Jesus as her Lord and Savior.

After we had prayed together, she lifted her head and was the first to speak. With a shining and joyous countenance she exclaimed, "So this is what those two kids are so excited about!" I gladly answered in the affirmative, as we began to enjoy a spontaneous celebration of her newfound salvation.

We then commenced to interact for a prolonged period of time about the glories and realities of new life in Christ. We never did return to the stated reason for her visit, the untimely marriage of her daughter (which the Lord did eventually sort out). However, by God's grace, we did end up dealing effectually with the primary reason that He had sent this precious mother our way. He wanted to call her onto the path of discipleship. He wanted to save her soul, thereby enabling her to begin a walk with Him through time, right on into eternity.

Aspect #4: Concerned about Ongoing Discipleship

Again, when the Lord is allowed to be the counselor, He counsels regarding the path of discipleship. Thus, ongoing discipleship is another high priority issue that we are to be concerned about in each counseling situation. This implication comes from the all-encompassing commission of Jesus to *"Go, make disciples of all the nations."* This command would not only involve getting people on the path of discipleship, but also helping them follow Jesus down that path. In other words, in every counseling session, we are not only to be concerned about initial salvation, but about ongoing discipleship as well.

Therefore, as we are praying and listening to those who are enlisting our help, we are asking the Lord to clarify this matter. If they already know the Lord, we want Him to show us if they desire to live as His disciples. If so, we can then encourage them to follow Jesus down His path for their lives. If they are not walking in this manner, God's priority for them would be to give immediate and substantial attention to ongoing discipleship. The Lord is not merely interested in having troubled souls find a renewed measure of comfort or relief. He wants to take whatever is causing them to seek help and use it to move them into a life of discipleship.

What will indicate where the heart is on this critical matter? A brief reminder from Luke 9:23 will supply us with the necessary insight:

> *"Then He said to them all, 'If anyone desires to come after Me, let him deny himself, and take up his cross daily, and follow Me'."*

As was noted earlier in Chapter Two, following Jesus as a disciple involves a daily willingness to say no to the independent self-life and to embrace the cross of Christ as our own personal instrument of death for the self-life. These terms of discipleship leave only one option for life, following Jesus to find in Him all that we need for true living.

At times in counseling situations, Christians may be consumed with conversation about the "**unholy trinity**" (**me, myself, and I**). Such improper focus can be ascertained through the repetition of a variety of self-centered, self-serving comments. "I don't like what I am getting out of all of this." "This is not fair to **me**." "I am not going to let anyone treat **me** like that." "I am going to take charge **of this entire matter myself**." "I can't trust anyone but **myself** anymore." Such statements demonstrate a serious absence of saying no to self and death to self, that Jesus Christ might be followed as Lord. It is probably time to have some straightforward biblical consideration of ongoing discipleship, through verses like: Luke 9:23; Romans 12:1-2; 1 Corinthians 6:19-20; 2 Corinthians 5:14-15; and Colossians 3:17.

Self-centered believers who respond to God's word regarding ongoing discipleship will certainly see the Lord at work in their current dilemmas. However, even more significantly, they will see the Lord operating in an increasingly comprehensive manner throughout all areas of their lives.

Aspect #5: Anticipating the Sharing of Scripture

Since the Lord is the Wonderful Counselor,

and since He counsels through His word, sharing scripture is to be the paramount aspect of any counseling situation. While reflecting upon a joint counseling session, my friend and associate, John, remarked, "Bob, you certainly do get people into the scriptures more rapidly than I do." I thought for a minute and replied, "John, I get folks into the word more rapidly than I formerly did."

Through the years in counseling, I have come to anticipate more and more earnestly the moment when I can open up the word of God and read it to a seeking heart. This is the occasion when the Wonderful Counselor is allowed to function in a role that He alone can properly fulfill. This is the opportunity for the sufficiency of scripture to be unleashed in people's lives, as elaborated upon previously in Chapter Four.

As I am listening and praying in any counseling situation, I ask the Lord to let me know what He wants to say to those who desire help. Whenever verses from scripture are brought to my mind, I consider that a direct work of the Holy Spirit answering my prayer.

> *"But the Helper, the Holy Spirit, whom the Father will send in My name, He will teach you all things, and bring to your remembrance all things that I said to you"* (John 14:26).

So, when the Spirit brings to my remembrance a passage of scripture, I either make a mental note of it, or I write it down on a slip of paper, depending upon which is most appropriate. Then, whenever I am asked any question that requests my input on the issues being communicated, I begin to read the word of God from those portions of scripture that the Holy Spirit has caused me to recall. A Spirit-led consideration of God's word is what sets true biblical counseling a world apart from man's opinions and suggestions and theories. These moments of unfolding the word of God directly into troubled or searching hearts are the priceless, pivotal, life-impacting times that we are to anticipate as we counsel God's way.

A word of caution and encouragement might be beneficial at this point. Too often, God's people disqualify themselves from being used of God in personal ministry, because they think that their memory is not acceptable. They fear that they will not be able to remember needed verses of the Bible. If God has gifted you with an outstanding memory, praise be to Him. He can certainly use your memory for His glory. However, the key to being used in counseling is not memory. Rather, it is the taking in of the word of the Lord, permitting the Holy Spirit to teach us from the whole counsel of God. Then, as we make ourselves available to serve, the Spirit will appropriately *"bring to our remembrance"* what He has already taught us.

Notice, **previously taught truth** is what the Holy Spirit brings to our remembrance. Personal consumption of, and response to, the word of God is what causes a growing reservoir of truth to develop in our hearts. This inner accumulation of heavenly realities is what the Spirit draws upon for ministry to others. Consequently, we want to be those who habitually receive the scriptures into our lives.

Aspect #6: Watching for Obvious, Necessary Responses

Another unfolding aspect of counseling situations is being alert to any obvious response that is necessary in the life of those who are seeking direction. Many matters that struggling people take to others for help are not complicated issues in the light of the word of God. Matthew 5:23-24 provides a clear illustration of this point:

> *"Therefore if you bring your gift to the altar, and there remember that your brother has something against you, leave your gift there before the altar, and go your way. First be reconciled to your brother, and then come and offer your gift."*

Imagine someone pouring out his heart to you concerning his inability to freely offer worship and praise to the Lord. Next, he reveals that whenever he attempts to worship God, he is haunted by thoughts of some person he has grievously wronged. This troubled seeker does not need months of introspective conjecture about why he cannot worship God more wholeheartedly. Instead, he needs to pursue an immediate course of action to reconcile with the person he has treated improperly.

Now, envision a person sharing with you about heavy torment that is going on relentlessly in his mind. He cannot eat or sleep or concentrate due to the incessant anguish that dominates his thoughts. Then, he discloses that he has been consistently engaged in a secret life of lying or cheating or fornicating. Again, such a person does not need months of personality testing to see why he cannot function with a clear mind. He needs to respond without delay to some forthright commands in the word of God.

"Flee sexual immorality" (1 Corinthians 6:18).

"Flee also youthful lusts; but pursue righteousness, faith, love, peace with those who call on the Lord out of a pure heart" (2 Timothy 2:22).

"Beloved, I beg you as sojourners and

pilgrims, abstain from fleshly lusts which war against the soul" (1 Peter 2:11).

Aspect #7: Encouraging Meditation of Scripture

Frequently, when ministering to someone who is seeking our help, we realize that it is going to be appropriate to get together again soon. Suggesting portions of scripture to meditate upon during the intervening days can be very productive. The most likely selection of Bible passages to suggest will be those that the Holy Spirit brought to our remembrance while we were listening and praying during the counseling session. These passages can be useful in future sessions with that person, as we spend time considering together what God was saying to him during his times of private reading and meditation. In addition, these passages can be invaluable in helping him develop a proper perspective on his long-range path of discipleship, which should involve hearing from the Lord personally and regularly through His word.

Our goal in counseling others is to be used of God to get His word into their lives, so that He may counsel them. If the word of God is given consistent attention between counseling sessions, the way is wide open for the Lord to be counseling that seeking heart day by day. Whenever a person hears from the Lord through His word without us present, we can later explain to him about how appropriate this process is in his daily walk as a disciple of Jesus Christ. Our desire for those we counsel is that they develop the same attitude and involvement with scripture that is expressed in Psalm 119:15-16 and 97:

> *"I will meditate on Your precepts, And contemplate Your ways. I will delight myself in Your statutes; I will not forget Your word. Oh, how I love Your law! It is my meditation all the day."*

Another word of caution is timely at this point. Meditating can be very dangerous, if it is approached man's way and not God's way. Characteristically, man's way of meditating has the wrong focus for the mind, or perhaps worse, no focus at all. Often, psychological theories of meditation consist of focusing the mind on self, imagining all the things that self desires to have or to do or to become. At best, this is a spiritual distraction, since God is looking for disciples who will deny self and follow Him. At other times, New Age meditation philosophies involve emptying the mind in order to receive new thoughts and ideas. Such a passive and subjective practice can leave people vulnerable to influence from the world, the flesh, or even the devil.

Biblical meditation necessitates actively thinking and reflecting upon the objective content of the word of God. It involves concentrating upon what God is saying in His word. Concurrently, we are to prayerfully ask Him to grant us true understanding, coupled with His personal application of that truth in our lives. The Spirit will use such godly meditation to provide the counsel, as well as produce the consequent life, that is declared in Psalm 1:1-3:

> "Blessed is the man Who walks not in the counsel of the ungodly, Nor stands in the path of sinners, Nor sits in the seat of the scornful; But his delight is in the law of the LORD, And in His law he meditates day and night. He shall be like a tree planted by the rivers of water, That brings forth its fruit in its season, Whose leaf also shall not wither; And whatever he does shall prosper."

Aspect #8: Praying about the Situation Persistently

The last unfolding aspect of the counseling situation that we will consider is praying persistently about that situation. In part, this is a repeat of the first aspect that we examined. Yet, it is more than mere repetition, even though there is great value in simply repeating important truths. Initially, we stressed praying about the counseling situation as it approached, as it began, and as it developed. Here, we will emphasize persistency in prayer.

"Pray without ceasing" (1 Thessalonians 5:17).

"Then He spoke a parable to them, that men always ought to pray and not lose heart" (Luke 18:1).

"Praying always with all prayer and supplication in the Spirit, being watchful to this end with all perseverance and supplication for all the saints" (Ephesians 6:18).

"Continuing earnestly in prayer, being vigilant in it with thanksgiving" (Colossians 4:2).

Too often, the tendency is to cease praying about a counseling situation before God is finished with the full work that He desires to do. Many times counseling needs will tempt us to give up and lose heart, when we instead should be seeking the Lord in prayer. Vigilant, earnest, and persistent prayer is perfectly designed for every counseling situation.

We not only want to pray before and during any counseling opportunity, we also want to pray as the session concludes, after it is over, and then for as many days as we sense the Lord laying it upon our hearts. Furthermore, we want to exhort the person seeking help to tenaciously lift up in prayer the issues that provoked the quest for counsel, as well as matters that God brought forth during time in the scriptures. In other words, saturating all counseling with much persistent prayer is a basic aspect of counseling God's way. Once again, the Lord is the Wonderful Counselor. In praying, we are continuing to place all matters into His hands that He might increasingly reveal and fully work out His perfect will, based upon His infinite wisdom and power and love.

Conclusion

These **guidelines for the counseling situation** are certainly not exhaustive or comprehensive in scope. Nonetheless, they are biblically fundamental and are, therefore, reliable and fruitful, when entered into with dependence upon the Holy Spirit. In looking for insights to equip us and make us more effective in counseling one another, we need unpretentious scriptural guidelines like these, rather than the sophisticated psychological theories of man.

So-Called Christian Counseling

During some thirty years of ministry, I have increasingly encountered so-called Christian counseling that neglected the biblical realities described above, while emphasizing the theoretical philosophies of man. Too many Christians offer or seek counsel based on subjective self-introspection, impotent self-help, and humanistic self-justification. Any counsel that neglects prayer, minimizes scripture, or overlooks discipleship is not counseling God's way.

Summary of Section Three

The word of God gives us clear direction concerning **who is to counsel** and **how they are to be equipped**. **All believers in general** are to participate in the personal ministry of sharing God's counsel with one another. Some will prove to have special spiritual gifting in this area, and will thereby be more effective than others. Some will have a more distinctive calling to counseling, and will therefore invest more time in it than others. Progressively, all will become fruitful in this ministry as they mature in their lives in Christ.

Equipping all believers for counseling one another is to come from within the biblically-ordained pathway that God has set in place for all spiritual service. This applies to the family of God in general, as well as to the specially gifted and distinctively called counselors in particular.

This pathway will include participation in the life of **the church** (Romans 14:19), under the spiritual guidance and development of **God's appointed leaders** (Ephesians 4:11-12). Primarily, it will incorporate **equipping in and by the word of God** (2 Timothy 3:16-17), with a major emphasis upon **growing in God's grace** and in an **acquaintanceship with Himself** (2 Peter 3:18). Such preparation for ministry also unfolds **vital biblical issues** useful in most counseling situations, even when specific guidelines on particular circumstantial matters may not be readily apparent. Saints equipped in this manner become more and more like the Lord Jesus Christ. Consequently, they counsel more and more as the Wonderful Counselor intends.

Let's seek the Lord to equip us to minister to one another in the manner that He desires, using the equipping means that He has ordained.

SECTION FOUR

Foundational Truths for Counseling

Now, we will consider the strategic role that **foundational biblical truths** can fulfill in counseling God's way. This subject enables us to consider the very heart of the spiritual realities that God uses to radically change lives. John 8:31-32 points us in this direction:

"If you abide in My word, you are My disciples indeed. And you shall know the truth, and the truth shall make you free."

As we previously observed in these verses, all of the truth of the word of God provides liberating power for people's lives. Now, we will contemplate another critical fact. Not all the truth of God's word is designed to have an impact of equal depth or comprehensive breadth upon lives. Some of the truths in the Bible are **foundational**. **All** of the Christian life is to be built upon them and affected by them. Similarly speaking, some biblical truths are **central**. **Every** aspect of the walk of a disciple is to be developed around them and related to them. Other truths in the word of God are non-foundational, non-central.

A Non-Foundational Truth

Proverbs 21:9 gives a good example of truth that is not foundational:

"It is better to dwell in a corner of a housetop, than in a house shared with a contentious woman."

Since the Lord included this in Proverbs, we know that this statement is both true in general, as well as particularly important in some lives at certain times. Nevertheless, we would never sit down with new disciples and tell them that developing a godly Christian walk is all tied up in this truth. Neither would we expect this verse to be included in a class designed for hungry, maturing believers, entitled: "The Essential Elements of Christian Growth and Service." The reason for omitting this verse from such a class is that the truth it states is non-foundational.

Counseling with Foundational Truths

Counseling situations are consistently in danger of becoming mired down in circumstantial issues, coupled with a pursuit after non-foundational truths. People often dwell upon the perplexing or uncomfortable details of their lives, while looking for specific steps to reestablish a personal zone of comfort and peace. Even earnest disciples of Jesus can get exceedingly sidetracked with a quest for Bible verses that satisfy a "when this occurs, do this" mentality.

Offering specific biblical insight for particular needs certainly has its place in counseling God's way. However, we do not want that type of ministry to eclipse this more essential approach of sharing foundational truths with those who come to us for counseling. **Imparting foundational truths** to others will not only help them get through their present difficulty, but it can also assist them in developing a more Christ-like life in general. Many people wrestle with so many impossible matters within them and around them, that a lifetime of non-foundational truth will not impact them sufficiently. Yet, being counseled in a few areas of foundational truths could ultimately impact virtually every area of their lives.

The foundational truths that we will examine in this section are four in number: **identification with Christ, who we are in Christ, the renewing of the mind,** and **spiritual warfare**. If we will seek the Lord for understanding of these truths and for a growing walk in these truths, He will then use us to minister these glorious realities to others who come to us seeking help and direction in life.

"For if by the one man's offense death reigned through the one, much more those who receive abundance of grace and of the gift of righteousness will reign in life through the One, Jesus Christ." — Romans 5:17

Chapter 12
Identification Truths of Romans 5-8

Identification truths in the word of God can seem profoundly inspiring, yet exceedingly elusive. The scriptures link these truths with an abundance of desirable spiritual realities, like victory and fruitfulness and wholeness. Yet, walking in these truths can appear to be impractical or unworkable.

The term **identification** is typically used by Bible teachers and biblical theologians in reference to **believers being united with Christ** (Romans 6:5) or **joined to Christ** (1 Corinthians 6:17). It is inherently related to that simple but extraordinary phrase **"in Christ"** (Ephesians 1:3).

Within these identification truths is all that is available to every person who has come to spiritually reside in Christ by saving faith in the Lord Jesus. What every believer needs is to learn of all that is ours in Christ and to walk in those wondrous provisions. Chapters five through eight of Romans speak of these very issues in a distinctively compelling manner.

In Adam or In Christ

Chapter five of Romans presents the critical issue of being "in Adam" or "in Christ." All the problems and troubles of humanity are related to being in Adam. All the remedies and resources of God for man are related to being in Christ. Romans 5:12 begins to unfold these matters:

> *"Therefore, just as through one man sin entered the world, and death through sin, and thus death spread to all men, because all sinned."*

In Adam, Man's Problems

Through one individual, Adam, sin entered the world. Adam's rebellion against God brought sin and death into the world. This death was not just physical. More critically, it involved spiritual death, a separation from God, with all of the spiritual deadness that brings. Then, from generation to generation, this death spread to all who were identified with Adam: namely, all of humanity. This is the reason why lives are so bound and broken. Mere personal circumstances are not the basic problem.

Evaluating people's personal circumstances is the typical approach to explaining difficulties in life. God's word goes past such temporal, visible issues and gets right to the timeless, unseen cause of all the problems among mankind. The sin that started with Adam has been passed on to everyone who was or is related to Adam through natural physical birth. Adam sired a race of sinners, rebels who serve self instead of God.

In Adam, man's nature is the problem, not just his behavior. Consequently, psychological counseling, which can only hope for a modification of behavior, is unable to offer to man what he really needs. People need to obtain a new parentage, a new life source. Counseling based upon psychological theory can only attempt to make Adam's race a bit more functional. Whereas, man needs to partake of an entirely new life, a life not dominated by sin and spiritual death. Such a life is to be found in Christ alone.

In Christ, God's Remedies

Romans 5:17 briefly restates the sin problem man faces in Adam, and then proceeds to describe the full remedy God provides in Christ:

> *"For if by the one man's offense death reigned through the one, much more those*

who receive abundance of grace and of the gift of righteousness will reign in life through the One, Jesus Christ."

Again, Adam's rebellion against God is mentioned. Through that sin death has reigned over the family of man. This is why the world in general and individuals in particular become so devastated. A tyrant dictator called death is ruling over the affairs of all who are identified with Adam. Behind this impersonal term, death, is the operation of the enemy of men's souls, *"the god of this age"* (2 Corinthians 4:4). His devastating influence encourages selfishness, dishonesty, fear, doubt, brutality, unfaithfulness, perversion, indulgence, wars, prejudice, apathy, abuse, addiction, pride, fornication, hatred, and even more. Yet, there is a remedy that is *"much more"* than sufficient to handle these dreadful signs of spiritual deadness.

*"**Much more** those who receive abundance of grace and of the gift of righteousness will reign in life through the One, Jesus Christ."*

Two heavenly realities are listed here which will enable people to increasingly live as Christ-like overcomers, walking in spiritual victory and vitality. These two are the *"gift of righteousness"* and the *"abundance of grace."* One of these two is known by every person who is no longer "in Adam," but is now "in Christ" through faith in Him. The other is sadly unknown by many true believers.

The *"gift of righteousness"* is the one every follower of Jesus is aware of, or else he is not a disciple of the Lord. The gift of righteousness allows sinful sons of Adam to stand before a holy God. Those who put their faith in Jesus Christ become those who are identified with Christ. They are placed in Christ, spiritually speaking. They are born again into the family of God. They are accepted by God on the basis of the righteousness of Christ, which is theirs as a gift from God. This describes everyone who is in Christ. Anyone who approaches the Lord on any other condition is still in Adam's family of fallen, sinful humanity.

"Abundance of grace" is the divine resource that too many believers neglect. Having the gift of righteousness does not automatically cause the children of God to live as victorious overcomers. That gift only grants them a place in God's family, with the full resources of the Lord available to them. These abundant resources of God's grace must be appropriated personally and consistently in order to *"reign in life through the One, Jesus Christ."*

So often, believers in Jesus Christ think of grace as being identical to forgiveness. We know that God has forgiven us by His grace, and we are so grateful that He did. However, we overlook the grand fact that His grace is far more than forgiveness alone. Forgiveness was merely our first life-giving drink from His ocean of abundant grace. As with *"the gift of righteousness,"* forgiveness alone does not produce a victorious Christian experience.

Grace for Victory and Service

To reign in life through Christ, we must by faith draw daily upon the abundance of grace that is found in Christ. In that heavenly ocean of grace, which contains **"the unfathomable riches of Christ"** (Ephesians 3:8, KJV), there is more than forgiving grace. There is also grace for growing, for serving, for bearing fruit, for abounding in good works, for being transformed, for living victoriously.

Paul was an example of one who consistently and humbly depended upon the abundance of God's grace in daily life and service. His testimony in 1 Corinthians 15:10 reveals that God's grace was the divine dynamic at work in His life that made him the effective and victorious Christian that he became:

> *"But by the grace of God I am what I am, and His grace toward me was not in vain; but I labored more abundantly than they all, yet not I, but the grace of God which was with me."*

United with Christ

Chapter six of Romans builds upon this glorious blessing of abundant grace available in Christ by depicting believers as being united with Christ:

*"Or do you not know that as many of us as were baptized into Christ Jesus were baptized into His death? Therefore we were buried with Him through baptism into death, that just as Christ was raised from the dead by the glory of the Father, even so we also should walk in newness of life. For if we have been **united together** in the likeness of His death, certainly we also shall be in the likeness of His resurrection, knowing this, that our old man was crucified with Him, that the body of sin might be done away with, that we should no longer be slaves of sin"* (Romans 6:3-6).

Knowing the Facts

"Do you not know?" These are facts that we are to know. Some portions of the scriptures are heavenly facts that we need to know in order to live God's way here on earth. Such verses are among the most foundational of all in God's word. These passages are perplexing to most of us at first, because they disclose things that God has done on our behalf.

Generally, we seem to more easily relate to instructions concerning things God commands us to do on His behalf, for His glory and honor and service. However, in order to work for God, we must first know of the work that He has already accomplished for us.

These verses reveal that all followers of the Lord have been *"baptized into Christ Jesus,"* that is, **identified with Him**. We have been *"united together"* **with Him, joined to Him, made one with Him**. We fully benefit from Him and partake in what He went through at the cross and the resurrection. His spiritual history becomes our spiritual history before the Father. As Adam acted on behalf of all related to him by natural, physical birth, so Christ acted on behalf of all related to Him by supernatural, spiritual birth. His death and resurrection become ours. At the cross, we died with Him. In the resurrection, we were raised with Him to *"walk in newness of life."* These are glorious facts that we are to know.

The Death of Our Old Self

The death of our old man, our old self, is an essential aspect of these great identification truths that we are to know. Our old, independent self-life was executed upon the cross of Jesus Christ. Consider again Romans 6:6:

> *"Knowing this, that our old man was crucified with Him, that the body of sin might*

*be done away with, that we should no
longer be slaves of sin."*

Everyone begins in Adam's family as a
slave of sin. All who have been born only
once, into Adam's family, are bound to exist
under the slavery of sin. This is as true of the
respected chairman of the board as it is of the
reviled addict of cocaine. Nevertheless, thanks
be to God, there is a way to *"no longer be
slaves of sin."* Freedom from sin's dominion
necessitates a spiritual liberation from *"the
body of sin."* If we are to *"no longer be slaves
of sin,"* the body of sin must *"be done away
with,"* literally, *"rendered powerless."*

God created people to be alive in their
spirits, able to relate and respond to Him, as
Adam and Eve did before their sinful rebellion. This spiritual life was to be expressed
through the soul of man, through his mind
and emotions and will, through his personality. This immaterial reality of human experience was to reside in a physical body that did
what it was told to do.

However, man rebelled, and his spirit
died. Since then, these human bodies, wherein sin dwells, have been exerting a controlling
influence upon Adam's race. Man's profound
need is to have this body of sin removed from
its dominating position, have it *"done away
with,"* or *"rendered powerless."* To provide for
this need God supplies a radical remedy, one

that man and his speculative theories could never produce. God's drastic solution is the spiritual execution of the original tenant, the person who first lived in what had become our body of sin.

Illustrated by Humpty Dumpty

To illustrate the liberating remedy of God, let's reflect upon the story of the egg-shaped nursery rhyme character, Humpty Dumpty.

> *"Humpty Dumpty sat on a wall.*
> *Humpty Dumpty had a great fall.*
> *All the king's horses and all the king's men,*
> *Couldn't put Humpty together again."*

In our consideration, let Humpty portray Adam. Yes, there was a great fall of enormous consequences. The original "human egg" was splattered almost beyond recognition. Now, gathered around this marred and damaged egg are all of the king's horses and all of the king's men. They are trying their best to put Humpty back into his former condition.

Sigmund Freud can be seen there speculating over Humpty. He thinks that he has located an id and an ego and a super-ego. Surely, this will help to unscramble this mangled egg.

Carl Jung is there, making pronouncements of Jesus as an ancient archetype of a savior. Certainly, this will stir hope of some recovery.

Abraham Maslow has joined the crowd of experts. He is suggesting a humanly reasonable hierarchy of needs that promises to self-actualize Humpty, making him all that he can ever hope to be.

Many others are crowding in to assist; including Alfred Adler, Erich Fromm, B. F. Skinner, William James, and Carl Rogers. Yet none of them, with all of their self-centered theories and their self-help resources, can put Humpty together again.

Suddenly, the Lord God Almighty thunders forth a word of instruction. He commands all of the egg experts to stand back. He then proclaims that Humpty's only hope is to allow his shattered life to be executed upon the cross of His Son. Then, the Father will raise up with His Son a new Humpty, in place of the old shattered one. This new Humpty can then share in the whole, resurrected life of the Son of God.

This is what God offers to Adam's fallen and fractured family. Through faith in Christ, through identification with Him in His death and resurrection, the old man can be replaced by a new creature in Christ. The old man, being spiritually dead, was unable to say no to this body of sin. This new, spiritually alive person can increasingly learn to say no to this body of sin, thereby increasingly and practically rendering it powerless. Now, this new tenant, though still dwelling in a body of sin, need *"no longer be a slave of sin."* Through our identification with the Lord Jesus, we have been resurrected with Him into an entirely new spiritual life.

This is the hope that the people of God have and need to hear. Whatever may have

bound us before or held us down or torment-
ed our lives does not have to dominate us
now. Neither do we need to attempt to "**put
Humpty Dumpty back together again.**" We can
learn to leave Humpty Dumpty in the tomb.
We can be exploring that new life in Jesus
Christ and allow the old grave clothes from
Adam's sin and death to keep falling off.
That is truth in Christ that can set us free.

Psychological theories can never hope to
replace our old fallen life with an entirely new
life. The best that human speculations can ever
accomplish is a rearranging or reforming or
readjusting of the old life in Adam. Only the
Lord and His truth can provide a new, liberat-
ed, growing, abundant life in His Son. These
are biblical facts that God wants us to know.

Counting on the Facts

What are we to do with these facts?
Romans 6:11 tells us we are to count on them.
That is how we are to walk in the newness
of life that God has given to us in His Son.

> *"Likewise you also, reckon yourselves to be
> dead indeed to sin, but alive to God in
> Christ Jesus our Lord."*

In our death with Christ, our old life died
to sin. In our resurrection with Christ, we
were given a new life that could relate to God
and respond to Him. We are to "reckon" that

these things are so. We are to depend upon
their reality and their effectiveness. We are to
conclude that what God has already accomplished for us in Christ can truly prevent sin
from holding us in spiritual slavery.

This is another way of saying *"the just
shall live by faith"* (Romans 1:17). The children of God do not live by circumstance or
by feeling or by our best self-effort or by
some special knack of coping. *"The just shall
live by faith."* We live by believing in God
and the truths He tells us and the work that
He did on our behalf. If we are in Christ,
these declarations are true of us. We can
reckon them as such. We can rely upon them.
God has done these things for us in the work
of His Son. He is merely asking us to trust
Him. The more we live by faith in these realities, the more we will see God demonstrating
them to us in our experience.

Presenting Ourselves to God

As we are learning to count upon the
facts of what God has done for us in Christ,
we are increasingly enabled to present ourselves to God for His will and His purposes.
Romans 6:13 speaks of this matter:

> *"And do not present your members as
> instruments of unrighteousness to sin, but
> present yourselves to God as being alive
> from the dead, and your members as*

instruments of righteousness to God."

This is the decision that the new person in Christ desires to make. As new creatures in Christ, we want to say, "Here is my life, Lord; use it for righteousness' sake." As those alive unto God we can say: "Father, because of the work of your Son for me, I present myself to you. I say no to fleshly impulses. I do not want to go on presenting the members of my body to sin like I used to do. I say no to that, because I am a new person in Christ. Here is my life. I am alive from the dead. Take the members of my body, my very being, and use me as an instrument of righteousness."

Walking According to the Flesh

In chapters five and six of Romans, there is sufficient provision to have an *"abundant life"* throughout these days upon earth, as well as have an entrance *"supplied to you abundantly into the everlasting kingdom"* (2 Peter 1:11). So why is chapter seven of Romans necessary? In the conflicts of Romans 7, we learn experientially of our absolute need for the resources provided in Romans 6.

Romans 7 is about walking according to the flesh. It is about trying to please God by our own best effort, by drawing upon our own human resources inherited from Adam. This inappropriate and inadequate approach to the Christian life always eventuates in a fleshly struggle.

A Fleshly Struggle

Verses 18 and 19 depict some aspects of this painful struggle. Although we need not remain in this Romans 7 battle, it seems that every Christian passes through it. Many return to it periodically.

> *"For I know that in me (that is, in my flesh) nothing good dwells; for to will is present with me, but how to perform what is good I do not find. For the good that I will to do, I do not do; but the evil I will not to do, that I practice."*

As soon as we look to Christ as our Lord and Savior, the Spirit of God stirs within us a desire to please God by doing good and refraining from evil. Yet, as we attempt to be involved in good things and to avoid that which is evil, we sometimes find ourselves doing the very opposite of what we desire. The reason this can happen is that *"in me (that is, in my flesh) nothing good dwells."*

Jesus said, *"No one is good but One, that is, God"* (Mark 10:18). Our flesh, our own natural humanity, is not good. Any good in our lives must be a result of the work of the Spirit of God imparting His goodness into and through the new heart of a new creature in Christ Jesus. The good in our lives is that the

Son of God, the God who alone is good, dwells in our lives. Trying to be good on our own best effort is failing to draw upon the only good available to us. It is attempting to live independently, without relying upon *"Christ in us,* (our) *hope of glory"* (Colossians 1:27). Such fleshly striving to please God, to live up to the good and holy standards of God, will find us in the Romans 7 struggle.

Many times through the years in numerous counseling situations, folks have poured out this anguished cry: "I want to please God. I set out to please God. Yet, all the things I don't want to do, I do. On the other hand, the great plans I have for pleasing God go undone?!" On many of these occasions, when I would open my Bible and read Romans 7:18 and 19, they could hardly believe that I was reading from the word of God. They would often exclaim, "Why, that is exactly where I am!" Undoubtedly, this is why God allowed this testimony of the Apostle Paul to be included in the scriptures. The Lord knew that we would be there some day ourselves.

This futile struggle is further related in verses 22 and 23.

> *"For I delight in the law of God according to the inward man. But I see another law in my members, warring against the law of my mind, and bringing me into captivity to the law of sin which is in my members."*

Oh, what a battle can rage inside of the mind! Conflicting forces exist inside each one of us who knows the Lord. Within our new hearts, there resides a Spirit-sent love for the perfect will of God, revealed in His holy law. This godly delight in the law cannot develop in the inner man of an unbeliever, because his spirit is dead toward the things of God. Yet, once the Lord comes to dwell in our lives, a delight in His ways begins to grow within us.

In opposition to this love for the things of God, there also exists *"another law in my members."* Within our natural human bodies, including the physical organ of the brain, there is the tendency toward sin that we inherited from Adam, called *"the law of sin which is in my members."* One of the critical truths concerning the resulting battle is that we cannot win the victory by relying on our own resources. Left to our best personal devices, this "other law" that wars against our desire to please God will *"bring us into captivity to the law of sin which is in our members."*

Same Old Bodies from Adam

All of this conflict relates to Christians having the same physical bodies that we had before we were saved. We are new tenants living in the same old tents. Upon believing in the Lord Jesus we received a new spirit and were born again as new creatures in Christ.

Thereafter, our souls (our minds and emotions and wills) can be in the process of being made new by the daily transforming work of God within us.

None of these realities affect the body that we received through Adam's line. Romans 8:23 says that *"even we ourselves* (Christians) *groan within ourselves, eagerly waiting for the . . . redemption of our body."* We are agonizing under the burden of living with a body, and therefore with a brain, that is prone to sin. This body will remain the same body until we are with the Lord Jesus, *"who will transform our lowly body that it may be conformed to His glorious body"* (Philippians 3:21). Later on, in chapter fourteen, we will examine another critical, related matter: the renewing of the mind.

A Humble Cry for a Deliverer

Here is a strategic truth. You and I cannot win the fight against the flesh by our own best effort. Flesh cannot defeat the flesh. The new creature in Christ is designed to live by sharing in the life of another, by drawing upon the life of the Lord Jesus Christ. Consequently, whenever a believer is caught in the throes of the struggle to please God by his own resources, the only way out is a humble cry for a deliverer. Romans 7:24-25 makes this point in a thoroughly evident manner:

"O wretched man that I am! Who will deliver me from this body of death? I thank God - (it is) - through Jesus Christ our Lord!"

Any believer who is willing to humbly declare his own spiritual bankruptcy and cry out for one who can rescue him will soon be singing a song of thanksgiving to God for the delivering work of Jesus Christ our Lord! Note however, the flesh-crucifying disposition of this humble plea for help. *"O wretched man that I am."* This is a confession of being utterly inadequate to function as our own deliverer.

Notice that this humble Romans 7 plea is an intensified application of the Luke 9:23 discipleship confession that we are to make daily.

"Then He said to them all, 'If anyone desires to come after Me, let him deny himself, and take up his cross daily, and follow Me'."

Every day we are to deal radically with the self-life that wants to impede our progress as a disciple of Jesus Christ. We are to say no to that independent human life, even death to it, that we might find life in Jesus alone. This clears our path of self-obstructions, that we might "follow Him." Whenever we neglect this path of dying to self, we eventually find ourselves in the Romans 7 struggle of *"walking according to the flesh."* This is when the Lord wants us to deeply face and profoundly deny the resources of the flesh. *"O wretched man that I am"* states the actual situation in a spiritually precise and humbling manner.

Psychological Substitutes for Wretchedness

Across the country, multitudes of God's redeemed children, trapped in the Romans Seven struggle, seek help from Christian counselors, who are committed to integrating psychological theory with biblical truth. Instead of being encouraged to humble themselves before God through this flesh-mortifying biblical plea, these beleaguered saints are invited to substitute flesh-protecting and flesh-strengthening confessions. So, the troubled cry becomes, "O **dysfunctional** one that I am." Or, "O **codependent** one that I am." Or perhaps even more popular, "O **victimized** one that I am." No such plea can ever acceptably replace the desperate supplication God is eager to honor.

Substituting What for Who

Another tragic substitution is typically offered by psychologically inclined Christian counselors. "What" is allowed to displace "Who." The self-sufficient flesh of man loves to ask, "**What can I do** to get myself out of this difficulty?" Too many counselors are trained to give hundreds of self-satisfying false hopes, clothed in sophisticated, pseudo-scientific, psychological perspectives. So again, instead of people finding God's relief through humble dependence upon Him, they are off on another fleshly attempt at becoming their own deliverer.

God is waiting to hear the humble plea of, *"Who will deliver me from this body of death?"* He is not interested in what can be concocted by the fallen, self-dependent, sin-inclined brain that resides within *"this body of death."*

How sad it is that throngs of frustrated believers are coaxed to avoid the very prayer that will access God's abundant grace. At the same time, their struggling flesh is vainly encouraged and strengthened against the only path down which it must eventually proceed, if there is to be any true spiritual progress.

Jesus, Our Comprehensive Deliverer

What stands out above all of these issues is the role that Jesus is to fulfill uniquely and comprehensively as our deliverer. Christ wants to be our Total Deliverer. He delivered us from the penalty of sin, when He died on the cross. He will some day deliver us from the very presence of sin, when He comes again to take us to be with Him forever. Meanwhile,

He delivers us from the power of sin, when He is allowed to be the object of our hope. Nothing less than this will suffice. We need Christ's deliverance from the abject spiritual poverty of the flesh as much as we needed His deliverance from the guilt of sin.

The struggling souls who are crying out this humble plea of Romans 7:24 are the ones profoundly "reckoning" that they are only and exclusively *"alive unto God in Christ Jesus our Lord"* (Romans 6:11). These are the ones who will sing the grateful testimony, *"I thank God -* (deliverance is) - *through Jesus Christ our Lord!"* These are the people who are ready to walk according to the Spirit, to trust the Holy Spirit to make the resources of Jesus their present portion for victorious living.

Walking According to the Spirit

Romans 8:3-4 includes the two "walks" available to every disciple of Jesus Christ. Furthermore, they hold forth the astounding expectation that is ours, if we select God's intended choice.

> *"For what the law could not do in that it was weak through the flesh, God did by sending His own Son in the likeness of sinful flesh, on account of sin: He condemned sin in the flesh, that the righteous requirement of the law might be fulfilled in us*

who do not walk according to the flesh but according to the Spirit."

The weakness of the law of God is that mankind could not live up to its demands by the resources of fallen humanity. Thus, Jesus, the Son of God, came to earth as a sinless man to do what the law could never accomplish, that is, take care of the problem of sin and provide mankind a way to meet the requirements of the law. Jesus died to pay the debt that was incurred by our sins against God's law. Now, for all who have trusted in Him for cleansing from sin, there remains a day-by-day, step-by-step choice. Will we walk according to the flesh, the path of bondage and defeat described in Romans 7, or will we walk according to the Spirit, the path of liberty and victory described in Romans 8?

For those who are willing to walk according to the Spirit, *"the righteous requirement of the law"* can be increasingly, experientially fulfilled in their lives. This is an astounding potentiality, when one remembers the heavenly magnitude of the righteous requirement of the law. God's commandments demand that we be as perfect as the Heavenly Father (Matthew 5:48) in every way, particularly in holiness (1 Peter 1:15-16) and in love (Matthew 22:36-40). We can be growing in holy and loving Christlikeness, as we *"do not walk according to the flesh but according to the Spirit."*

The Law of the Spirit of Life in Christ Jesus

The reason why walking according to the Spirit has such a radical impact upon our experience can be seen in Romans 8:2:

> *"For the law of the Spirit of life in Christ Jesus has made me free from the law of sin and death."*

As we walk according to the Spirit, the greater spiritual principle of *"the law of the Spirit of life in Christ Jesus"* is functioning in our lives. During these times, we are being set free from the lesser spiritual principle of *"the law of sin and death."*

We are all familiar with the manner in which a greater law can overrule a lesser law in the realm of the physical world. A large intercontinental jet airliner provides a vivid example. Those huge planes are held down "in bondage" to the ground by what we could call a lesser law, the law of gravity. Unless a greater law is introduced, that impressive vessel has no hope of being "set free" to fly like a bird. Yet, whenever that land-bound giant is made subject to the greater law of aerodynamics, it can soar like an eagle through the sky.

Similarly, this is what takes place in the spiritual realm. Whenever we walk according to the Spirit, instead of according to the flesh, *"the* (greater) *law of the Spirit of life in Christ Jesus"* makes us *"free from the* (lesser) *law of sin and death."* Our walk of dependence upon the Holy Spirit allows the Spirit to supply us with the very life that is in Christ Jesus. This allows Christ to be our life practically at that time, as He is declared to be in Colossians 3:4 (*"Christ, who is our life"*). This is the only life that can be formed in us (Galatians 4:19) that can increasingly measure up to the holy law of God (Romans 8:4).

Incidentally, this is one of the great joys of counseling God's way. We can point people to a life that is whole, full, and free, Christ's life to be lived out in them. This is immeasurably superior to a life shaped by the humanistic theories of man.

Thus, the life of Christ can be genuinely operating in and through us. Instead of being held down in self-bondage by the spiritual gravity of the *"the law of sin and death,"* we are enabled to *"mount up with* (spiritual) *wings like eagles"* (Isaiah 40:31). We are given "(spiritual) *hinds' feet . . . to walk upon* (spiritually) *high places"* (Habakkuk 3:19). We are enabled to actually view life as those who have been seated *"in the heavenly places in Christ Jesus"* (Ephesians 2:6). These verses describe the fullness of life available in Christ to those *"who do not walk according to the flesh but according to the Spirit."*

Conclusion

Of the myriads of believers who are

searching for help through counseling, untold numbers are involved in extensive evaluation of their behavioral agonies or circumstantial pains. Many of these anticipate that some procedural steps or psychological insights will bring them success in their quest for fullness of life. The vast majority of them could undoubtedly find monumental measures of godly assistance from consideration of these **foundational identification truths** found in Romans 5, 6, 7, and 8.

In these truths we have seen that all of man's problems are related to his beginning in the fallen family of Adam's race. Conversely, all of God's remedies for man are found in the provisions available in Christ. The Lord deals with the old man in Adam through the cross of His Son. Then, He creates in Christ a new man through a **uniting with Christ** in His resurrection. This new creation has the abundant riches of God's grace made fully accessible to him in Christ.

However, even though we are made one with Christ and can live by His sharing of His life with us, we still have **a constant choice** that must be exercised. We must decide continually whether we will **walk by the flesh**, depending upon man's natural capacities, or **walk by the Spirit**, relying upon God's supernatural resources. Those who walk in dependence upon the Spirit of God increasingly grow in Christlikeness, as Jesus imparts His life into them and through them.

Such realities are **foundational** to the Christian life. As we stand upon them, and then share them with others in personal ministry, these truths can impact every area of a person's life simultaneously and increasingly. This is one of the great joys the Lord has given to us in counseling God's way.

"Therefore, if anyone is in Christ, he is a new creation, old things have passed away; behold, all things have become new." — 2 Corinthians 5:17

Chapter 13
Who We Are in Christ

As we continue to consider **foundational truths** for counseling God's way, we will again see that such truths are central and formative. As we learn to depend upon them, they can impact many areas of a person's spiritual life concurrently.

Who we are in Christ is another significant aspect of this type of truth. Once again, this is a common motivating factor in the lives of those who seek counseling. People want to know who they are. Some people engage in perplexing and even bizarre behavior, attempting to discover what their identity might be. To accurately and thoroughly find out who we are, we need the Lord Himself to tell us. God addresses these issues fully in His word.

The Old Identity in Adam

In the scriptures, the identity of the unsaved, all who are in Adam, is clearly defined and completely dreadful.

> *"And you He made alive, who were dead in trespasses and sins, in which you once walked according to the course of this world, according to the prince of the power of the air, the spirit who now works in the sons of disobedience, among whom also we all once conducted ourselves in the lusts of our flesh, fulfilling the desires of the flesh and of the mind, and were by nature children of wrath, just as the others"* (Ephesians 2:1-3).

Unless and until people come to know Jesus Christ as Lord and Savior, they are spiritually dead and under the control of Satan. They are characterized by indulgence and disobedience. By their very essence they deserve wrath and engender wrath. Truly, this is a tragic identity for all who are not in Christ.

New Creatures in Christ

Conversely, those who are found in Christ receive an entirely new identity. 2 Corinthians 5:17 declares this wondrous fact decisively:

> *"Therefore, if anyone is in Christ, he is a new creation; old things have passed*

away; behold, all things have become new."

Followers of the Lord Jesus are not the same people we were before meeting Him. We are not who others say we are. We are not who our emotions tell us we are. We are who God says we are, now that we are in Christ. Since we now live in Christ and upon His resources, we are who God has made us to be, based upon who Jesus is and all that He has accomplished for us.

Everyone who is in Christ is a new creation. In our standing before God, we are new spiritual beings. We have been born again by the Spirit of God from above. Yes, we still live in the same old physical tents. True, we still must contend with what was logged in our old physical brains. Nevertheless, we are new tenants in these old bodies.

We have been given a new life in the Lord, and we can now *"serve in the newness of the Spirit"* (Romans 7:6). As far as God is concerned, our old life, character, and destiny are gone, and *"all things have become new."* We cannot develop our lives through the psychological theories of man. Such theories typically emphasize a backward-looking examination of the old dead things in our old dead existence. It is from our new life in Christ and our new identity in Him that we want to learn to walk. As Romans 6:4 puts it, *"just as Christ was raised from the dead by the glory of the Father, even so we also should walk in newness of life."* In light of our new identity, we can walk in this new manner.

Branches in the Vine

In our old dead state of being in Adam, we had no sufficient resource to draw upon for true living. Now, in Christ, we are branches in the vine.

> *"I am the vine, you are the branches. He who abides in Me, and I in him, bears much fruit; for without Me you can do nothing"* (John 15:5).

Now that we are in Christ, it is such a simple matter to find out who we are. We merely ask the One who created us, redeemed us, and placed us in Christ. He then tells us in forthright language through His word: *"You are the branches."*

The Lord gives us such insights into our spiritual identity so that we might know how to relate to Him and, thereby, bring glory and honor to Him. Notice how these divine purposes are marvelously achieved in the vine and branches revelation.

Every physical branch must find in the vine all that is needed for an abundant and fruitful life. The branch need not, indeed cannot, supply its own life. The branch cannot produce any fruit on its own. Yet, the life of the vine can flow through the branch and produce abundant fruit that is characteristic of the life that is in the vine.

This is exactly what the Lord has in mind for us as spiritual branches. We do not innately have life in ourselves as branches. Thus, it is imperative that we look to our vine for the abundant life that He wants us to have. Apart from Jesus, we are unable to do anything that is of eternal value, that is genuinely Christlike, that can impact lives for God's kingdom, or that can bring honor and glory to Him.

On the other hand, if we will live in dependence upon our vine, His life will flow through us, by the work of the Holy Spirit. The result will be true spiritual fruit in our lives produced by Him and characteristic of Him, not produced by us and characteristic of us. Such an abiding life will display the fruit of *"love, joy, peace, longsuffering, kindness, goodness, faithfulness, gentleness, self-control"* (Galatians 5:22-23).

Think of the implications of this truth. All that we need as branches in the vine, all that we hunger for, all that we yearn to walk in and know and become, is already there in the vine. Everything God has demanded of us, everything He wants us to be, is all right there in the vine. If we just abide in Him, walk with Him, count on Him, look to Him, hope in Him, that life of His will come forth through us. Being who we now are in Christ, branches in the vine, makes such fruitfulness our normal expectation.

Complete in Christ

Closely related to being branches in the vine is the fact that we are complete in Christ. Colossians 2:9-10 discloses this astounding reality:

> *"For in Him dwells all the fullness of the Godhead bodily; and you are complete in Him."*

Here is one of the amazing aspects of who we are in Christ. In Him, we have a life that is not partial or empty or missing any necessary elements. We have a life available to us that is whole and full and sound. Virtually every believer in Jesus would most likely say, "These terms do not describe me, because my life is lacking and fractured and defective." This would be a valid confession for all of us, if we were speaking about our self-life, the best life that our natural human resources could produce. However, this statement in Colossians 2 has nothing to do with what we are able to effect. The completeness of life mentioned therein is all about who Christ is and what He provides for us.

There resides in the Lord Jesus Christ the full supply of what the Godhead has for man.

Fullness of life is in Him. Since we are in Him, we are therefore complete in His fullness. We do not have to attempt to manufacture a whole life. Whenever we rely upon ourselves, we are accessing the fleshly, unacceptable life of Adam's defective race. The completeness of life that we need is already ours in Christ. Whenever we draw upon that life by faith in Him, we are appropriating wholeness of life. Once more, who we are in Christ is the basis for experiencing life abundant.

More of Who We are in Christ

There is so much more in the word of God concerning who we are in Christ. The following verses give some rich examples of these great truths:

*"For **we are God's fellow workers; you are God's field, you are God's building**"* (1 Corinthians 3:9).

*"Do you not know that **you are the temple of God** and that the Spirit of God dwells in you?"* (1 Corinthians 3:16)

*"Now **you are the body of Christ**"* (1 Corinthians 12:27).

*"**You are** manifestly **an epistle of Christ**"* (2 Corinthians 3:3).

*"For you were once darkness, but now **you***

are light in the Lord. Walk as children of light" (Ephesians 5:8).

"But you are a chosen generation, a royal priesthood, a holy nation, His own special people, that you may proclaim the praises of Him who called you out of darkness into His marvelous light" (1 Peter 2:9).

These declarations describe in part the very essence and identity of those who are disciples of the Lord Jesus and are thereby in Christ. We are co-laborers with each other and with God. We are the field in which He plants and grows His spiritual produce. We are the building, the temple, that He is constructing, that He might dwell therein. We are His hands, feet, arms, and voice in this world today. We are the living letters of His reality that people are reading daily. We are the vessels which shine forth into this dark world the light of heaven that He alone can radiate. We are God's chosen ones. We are priests in a divine monarchy. We are a kingdom set apart unto God. We are His very own possession.

All of these blessings, and many others as well, form our spiritual identity. They are true of us because of the person and work of the Lord Jesus Christ. They describe the heart of our very being as new creatures. This is so because we are in Christ, benefiting from His character and His provisions.

Each of these realities offers insight into

relating to the Lord, and they generate reasons for giving glory to Him. One thing that they do not do deserves a special warning.

Warning about "Back Door Self-Esteem"

It may be true that many of us have heard very little in our churches about who we are in Christ. This is a sad oversight at best. However, another sad development has accompanied this grand theme when it does get some appropriate attention in teaching. This lamentable situation is the way in which some hold forth our new identity in Christ as a means of **bringing self-esteem philosophy in through the back door** of the kingdom of God.

Jesus clearly and forcefully closed the front door of His kingdom on self-esteem.

> *"And when He had called the people to Him, with His disciples also, He said to them, 'Whoever desires to come after Me, let him deny himself, and take up his cross, and follow Me. For whoever desires to save his life will lose it, but whoever loses his life for My sake and the gospel's will save it' "* (Mark 8:34-35).

> *"He who loves his life will lose it, and he who hates his life in this world will keep it for eternal life"* (John 12:25).

All who would follow the Lord must be willing to say no to the independent self-life.

They must be willing to have it nailed to the cross. They must be willing to agree with God that any life we could produce and sustain by ourselves is a life to despise and renounce, not to love and esteem.

Nonetheless, some who teach about who we are in Christ, as well as some who hear it taught, use this theme as an erroneous springboard to self-esteem thinking. Some who teach about Christians having a new identity in Christ corrupt this message by saying, "Doesn't this make you feel good about yourself?" Some who hear of our new identity in Christ say, "I like this, because it enhances my view of myself." Such applications totally miss the point of God's word on this subject and tragically contaminate the intended results. Such thinking places **the focus on the wrong person**.

Exhortation about "Christ-Esteem"

This encouraging, instructive, and faith-building message of who we are in Christ should lead to **Christ-esteem**, not self-esteem. It should stir us to hold Him in high regard, not ourselves. This is true, because, even though we have **individual** identities, we no longer have **independent** identities.

Branches in a physical vine have individual identities. Each branch is distinguishable from the others. Members of a physical body have individual identities. An eye is easily differentiated from a foot or an ear or from any other member of the body. On the other hand, neither branches in vines nor members of physical bodies have independent identities. Detach a branch from its vine, and all living identity is gone. Likewise, remove the eye from the body, and all living identity is gone.

So it is with all of us who follow Jesus. Remove Jesus from our lives and all living identity is gone. As believers in Jesus Christ, **our identity is based upon our relationship with Him and all that He has done for us**.

Boasting in the Lord

We have been created as beings who yearn to boast in something. The natural tendency of fallen man, as well as the flesh of redeemed humanity, is to boast in things of self. We want to brag about **our** abilities, **our** family, **our** country, **our** sports team. Well, the scriptures tell us exactly where our boasting is to be aimed, and where it is not to be aimed.

> *"For consider your calling, brethren, that there were not many wise according to the flesh, not many mighty, not many noble; but God has chosen the foolish things of the world . . . and God has chosen the weak things . . . and the base things . . . and the despised . . . **that no man should boast before God**. But by His doing you*

*are in Christ Jesus, who became to us wis-
dom from God, and righteousness and
sanctification, and redemption, that, just
as it is written, 'Let him who boasts, boast
in the Lord' "* (1 Corinthians 1:26-31,
NASB).

There is much appropriate boasting to
be given concerning who we are in Christ,
but all such boasting must be directed toward
the Lord. In fact, 1 Peter 4:11 lets us know
that all glory for time and eternity is to go to
the Lord Himself:

*"If anyone speaks, let him speak as the ora-
cles of God. If anyone ministers, let him
do it as with the ability which God supplies, that **in all things God may be glorified through Jesus Christ, to whom belong
the glory and the dominion forever and
ever.** Amen."*

A Reflective Question

A question was asked some time ago at
one of the Counseling God's Way Seminars
that I have been conducting for years across
America and overseas. After hearing that the
back door of God's kingdom was also closed
to self-esteem thinking, someone asked with a
measure of frustration, "Well, where does that
leave us?" The inference was that we were
not being left in a very good place.

Actually, all of this truth about who we are in Christ, and all of the boasting and glory going to Him and not to us, leaves us in an outstanding position. It leaves us fully provided for, immeasurably blessed, completely secure, and eternally loved. It leaves us abundantly supplied with spiritual resources and fruitfully abounding in heavenly purposes. It leaves us humbled, overwhelmed, encouraged, expectant, and at peace. It leaves us praising the Lord, loving Him, seeking Him, serving Him, glorifying Him, and wanting to be focused totally on Him. The place it does not leave us is focused on ourselves.

Conclusion

For our spiritual growth and development, as well as for our personal ministry to others, **knowing who we are in Christ is strategic foundational truth.** These revelations from the Lord show us how to relate to Him and give us great reasons to praise and magnify Him. If we ask the Lord to establish us more in these truths, our entire walk with Him will be strengthened. Also, we will thereby be prepared to share these glorious realities with others who come to us looking for spiritual assistance.

One last thought is in order. Remember, for many of God's people, such truth will mark a completely new way to think. However, this is part of what **the renewing of the mind** is all about. This will be our **next foundational truth** to consider.

And do not be conformed to this world, but be
transformed by the renewing of your mind,
that you may prove what is that good and acceptable
and perfect will of God." — Romans 12:2

Chapter 14
The Renewing
of the Mind

God directs us in Romans 12:2 to *"be
transformed by the renewing of your mind."*
This touches upon **another crucial foundational
truth** for counseling God's way. **The renewing
of the mind** is a biblical issue that should be
given consistent attention in Christian living
and personal ministry. This involves learning
to think God's way, whereas we had formerly
filled our minds with man's way of thinking.
Without this truth, we and the people we minister to cannot be changed into what God wants
us to be. Conversely, as believers grow in this
transforming work of God, the impact can be
experienced simultaneously in multiple arenas

of spiritual development.

The Need for Minds to be Renewed

The stark description of the unredeemed mind in Ephesians 4:17-19 shows us why human minds so desperately need to be renewed:

> *"This I say, therefore, and testify in the Lord, that you should no longer walk as the rest of the Gentiles walk, in the futility of their mind, having their understanding darkened, being alienated from the life of God, because of the ignorance that is in them, because of the hardening of their heart; who, being past feeling, have given themselves over to licentiousness, to work all uncleanness with greediness."*

These accurate phrases depict humans who exist without a knowledge of God: *"The futility of their mind . . . having their understanding darkened . . . alienated from the life of God . . . the ignorance that is in them . . . the hardening of their heart . . . past feeling . . . given over to licentiousness . . . to work all uncleanness with greediness."* This is what characterized our thinking before we came to Jesus Christ. Our reasonings were vain and empty. There was no spiritual enlightenment in our comprehensions. We were isolated from God's life, from whence alone comes all true insight. In us dwelled an intrinsic spiritual ignorance. The inner core of our being resisted the things of heaven. We were calloused to the convicting work of the Spirit of God. Our lives were committed to indulgence, without godly restraint. With covetous motivations we plunged into profane pursuits. All of this emphatically indicates the desperate need we all have to find a new way of thinking, once we come to Jesus as our Lord and Savior.

As new creatures in Christ, each of us must contend with all that that was pumped into our physical brains by the "old man" that we once were in Adam. Memories from the old life, logged in our brains, can influence our perspectives now. Values and priorities, learned in the days before Jesus became our Lord and Master, tend to cloud our evaluations, as we consider how to please and serve Christ today. Wandering thoughts can easily drift into the unwholesome areas of worldly thinking developed over years of existing without Christ in our lives.

It is as though the previous tenant, our old man in Adam, painted the walls of our brains with gross, self-centered, flesh-indulgent murals. Then, we are born again and begin to live in the dwelling place of this physical tent, and we sense a radical need to do some major redecorating. These mental murals urgently need repainting. They are repainted as we increasingly and comprehensively learn to think God's way in all matters that we address.

Renewed Spirit of the Mind

One aspect of our minds that needs renewing is the general mind-set. In Ephesians 4:23 we are told to *"be renewed in the spirit of your mind."* The *"spirit of* (our) *mind"* involves the basic framework of our thinking, the basic disposition or focus or overall controlling perspective of our minds. This is a good place to begin in having our minds restored to their proper condition, that is, in having our minds functioning as God intended.

Contrasting examples can help us see what the Lord might want to do here. The spirit of some minds is very skeptical concerning the existence of God, while others are curious to learn some facts about Him. The basic disposition of mind in some people is they will admit only that God exists, while others are eager to know Him and respond to Him. The mind-set that God desires us to have includes both the acknowledgment that He exists as well as the yearning to become one who loves Him with all of our being. Any other "spirit of the mind" needs to be renewed unto this framework that pleases God.

Often, in personal ministry and counseling, the real problem is not the narrow circumstance or issue dominating their attention. Rather, they need to give consideration to a renewing of their basic mental framework, the *"spirit of* (their) *mind."* When the overall controlling perspective of our minds is wrong, our perception of every individual matter of thinking will be clouded. The great theme verses of Proverbs come to bear at this point.

> *"The fear of the LORD is the beginning of knowledge, but fools despise wisdom and instruction"* (Proverbs 1:7).

> *"The fear of the LORD is the beginning of wisdom, and the knowledge of the Holy One is understanding"* (Proverbs 9:10).

Unless the *"spirit of* (our) *mind,"* our basic mental disposition, includes a respectful, reverent acknowledging of the Lord God Almighty, we cannot even begin to operate by any real knowledge and wisdom.

Renewing All of the Mind

In Romans 12:1-2, the Lord takes the range of this subject far beyond the important issue of our mind-set and on into the entire scope of our thinking:

> *"I beseech you therefore, brethren, by the mercies of God, that you present your bodies a living sacrifice, holy, acceptable to God, which is your reasonable service. And do not be conformed to this world, but be transformed by the renewing of*

your mind, that you may prove what is that good and acceptable and perfect will of God."

Yes, we need to be renewed in the spirit of our minds. Yet further, we need every aspect of our minds renewed. *"And do not be conformed to this world, but be transformed by the renewing of your mind."* No limiting terms are introduced here. God's renewing work is to involve the entire mind.

Avoiding Conformity to This World

Followers of the Lord Jesus Christ are not to have their thinking molded and shaped by the world, by man's ways. *"Do not be conformed to this world."* This solitary injunction should be sufficient to prevent the Lord's church from patterning her counseling after the ideas of human psychological theoreticians.

Of course, this command is much larger than the issue of how we counsel. This command covers every area of a person's thinking, as well as how one's thinking shapes all of life in general. Those who are in the world, separated from Christ and His truth, have their lives molded by the thoughts of the world. Christians are not only to avoid worldly patterns of thinking and living, we are also to undergo a transformation from the old ways of man to the new ways of God.

Being Transformed

Instead of having the world shape us by external pressures, we are to have our lives made increasingly and genuinely new by the renewing of our minds. This process is an internal working of God. Through His word by the work of His Holy Spirit, the Lord gives us an entirely new way to think. Then, the more we learn to think the Lord's way in all areas of life, to that degree we have our lives transformed. In this process, God is developing within us a new heavenly set of understandings, values, priorities, and resources for living.

Sadly, many Christians never seem to have their lives significantly changed. They continue to live much like they did when they were dead in trespasses and sins. They still live by their wits. They still have self-made lives. Their confidence is not in God, but rather in themselves. Why is this so? The answer is right here in our present text. Such Christians are not having their minds renewed. They are still holding onto and living by many of their old ways of thinking. Consequently, they persist in talking, acting, and deciding much as they had typically done before.

Another question is in order: Why are some Christians not having their minds renewed? Again, our text offers the necessary insight. Such stagnant lives are not in the spiritual place where minds get renewed.

Living Sacrifices

The preceding verse indicates the spiritual setting in which minds can be made new: *"Present your bodies a living sacrifice, holy, acceptable to God."* The renewing of the mind occurs as one lives on the altar of God. Many believers wrongly assume that their lives are their own. They are unaware of, or have not responded to, the truth of 1 Corinthians 6:19-20:

> *"Or do you not know that your body is the temple of the Holy Spirit who is in you, whom you have from God, and you are not your own? For you were bought at a price; therefore glorify God in your body and in your spirit, which are God's."*

God redeemed our lives by the precious blood of His dear Son. We now belong to the Lord. When we view our lives as our own, we do not pursue earnestly after the mind of the Lord. We are willing to settle for lives directed by our own understanding. When we acknowledge God's ownership of our lives, we have a yearning to know what He desires to do with these lives that are really His, and not ours.

Yet another question is now warranted: Why is it that some Christians are not placing their lives on the altar of God, agreeing with Him about His ownership of their very existence? Once more, our text suggests the answer. They may be unaware of the appropriate biblical appeal that makes the altar of God the only spiritually reasonable place to lay down our lives.

The Mercies of God

God's appeal to us to become living sacrifices unto Him is based upon His great mercies. *"I beseech you therefore, brethren, by the mercies of God."* Throughout eleven chapters of this powerful epistle, the Lord unfolds His glorious mercies toward those who only deserve condemnation and judgment. An understanding of and appreciation for God's kind and gracious dealings with us is what stirs us to present ourselves to Him.

In chapter one, God's mercy is seen in *"the gospel of Christ,"* which is *"the power of God to salvation for everyone who believes"* (verse 16). In chapter two, His mercy is inferred through a piercing question:

> *"Or do you despise the riches of His goodness, forbearance, and longsuffering, not knowing that the goodness of God leads you to repentance?"* (verse 4).

Chapter three adds the merciful work of the Lord in His providing justification for us *"freely by His grace through the redemption that is in Christ Jesus"* (verse 24).

God's merciful ways are revealed in chapter four by linking faith, grace, and the promises of God: *"Therefore it is of faith that it might be according to grace, so that the promise might be sure to all the seed"* (verse 16). The redeemed, trusting heart can thereby rest in complete certainty regarding the promises of the Lord's saving work on his behalf.

Chapter five is overflowing with heavenly declarations of the mercy of God:

> *"We have peace with God through our Lord Jesus Christ, through whom also we have access by faith into this grace in which we stand"* (verses 1-2).

> *"The love of God has been poured out in our hearts by the Holy Spirit who was given to us"* (verse 5).

> *"For if by the one man's offense death reigned through the one, much more those who receive abundance of grace and of the gift of righteousness will reign in life through the One, Jesus Christ"* (verse 17). *"But where sin abounded, grace abounded much more"* (verse 20).

This one chapter alone offers divine, undeserved provisions for peace with God, access to grace, hearts filled with love, victory for living, and sufficient grace to cover (and to recover from) abounding sin!

In chapter six, further mercies are proclaimed, concerning freedom from the domination of sin:

> *"For sin shall not have dominion over you, for you are not under law but under grace"* (verse 14).

In chapter seven, God's mercy holds forth more freedom from the law:

> *"But now we have been delivered from the law, having died to what we were held by, so that we should serve in the newness of the Spirit and not in the oldness of the letter"* (verse 6).

Chapter eight stands out bold and rich in describing the mercies of God:

> *"For the law of the Spirit of life in Christ Jesus has made me free from the law of sin and death"* (verse 2).

> *". . . that the righteous requirement of the law might be fulfilled in us who do not walk according to the flesh but according to the Spirit"* (verse 4).

> *"But if the Spirit of Him who raised Jesus from the dead dwells in you, He who raised Christ from the dead will also give life to your mortal bodies through His Spirit who dwells in you"* (verse 11).

> *"For I consider that the sufferings of this present time are not worthy to be compared*

with the glory which shall be revealed in us" (verse 18).

"And we know that all things work together for good to those who love God, to those who are the called according to His purpose" (verse 28).

"He who did not spare His own Son, but delivered Him up for us all, how shall He not with Him also freely give us all things?" (verse 32).

"For I am persuaded that neither death nor life, nor angels nor principalities nor powers, nor things present nor things to come, nor height nor depth, nor any other created thing, shall be able to separate us from the love of God which is in Christ Jesus our Lord" (verses 38-39).

In chapters nine through eleven, God's mercy is proclaimed in His faithfulness toward Israel, His stubborn and stiff-necked people:

"Behold, I lay in Zion a stumbling stone and rock of offense, and whoever believes on Him will not be put to shame" (9:33).

"All day long I have stretched out My hands to a disobedient and contrary people" (10:21).

"The Deliverer will come out of Zion, and He will turn away ungodliness from Jacob" (11:26).

Only after an extended elaboration of God's glorious mercies toward all who believe is the appeal given to respond appropriately.

Your Reasonable Service

Since God has been so merciful to us, the only spiritually reasonable thing to do is to say, "Lord, here is my life; it is Yours to use as You please." No other response makes any sense at all. Nonetheless, we cannot coerce people to lay their lives upon the altar of God. We cannot effectively badger them to such a commitment. The Lord's compelling mercies soften the heart unto this necessary abandonment to Him.

This type of life undergoes a continual renewing of the mind. This is the person who develops a passion to be in the word of God, so that they might learn how to think His way more and more in every matter. Consequently, this is the Christian who will experience a transformed life, increasingly brought into line with the will of God, as revealed by the word of God.

Demonstrations of God's Will

Many believers seek the will of God only in times of difficulty or dilemma. Now, it is a wonderful thing when anyone at any time becomes concerned about God's will. However, there is a far better path available than a sporadic chasing after the will of God from crisis to crisis. Our lives can actually become a growing demonstration of that divine will.

The sequence that leads to such a delightful result is laid out here. First, the heart is touched by the magnitude of the mercies of God. Next, that worshiping life is placed upon the altar of God for His use and His glory. Then, the renewing of the mind can consistently proceed, as that person seeks to know what God wants to do with his life. More and more that life undergoes spiritual transformation, as his thinking is made increasingly like the Lord's. The result is a life that day by day demonstrates *"what is that good and acceptable and perfect will of God."*

Conclusion and Warning

Many people seeking a word of counsel from a family member, friend, church leader, or pastor need to discover God's provisions for producing changes in their lives. They would benefit immeasurably from **this foundational truth about the renewing of the mind**.

However, we should be alert to, and alert others about, counseling which sounds somewhat like the renewing of the mind, but is actually just a psychological mind game. One popular example of this would be the attempt to heal memories by visualizing Jesus entering into our bad memories and dealing with the situation and/or comforting us back there in the midst of it.

Such counseling approaches are often held forth as Christian, but are based upon a psychological mind-set. Trying to manipulate reality or develop it through the powers of our imagination involves drawing upon the resources of the flesh. This does not produce Christlikeness. Rather, it strengthens the self-life instead of considering it as dead.

Instead of humanistic groping through some type of "backwards imagining," the Lord desires to impact us today. He wants to touch us in the reality of our present living. **He intends for us to think as He thinks** about any past memories, any present experiences, and any future concerns. He wants to teach us to trust in Him now and to follow Him today. He desires to **renew our minds currently, by helping us to think His way** in every area of life.

"Put on the whole armor of God, that you may be able to
stand against the wiles of the devil."
— Ephesians 6:11

Chapter 15
Spiritual Warfare

Regarding **foundational truths**, we will
consider one more strategic arena, **spiritual
warfare**. Very often, those seeking counsel are
wondering why life can become so difficult,
hectic, or even impossible. Generally, the
underlying cause of such struggles is the fact
that human lives are lived out each day on a
battlefield. Three major biblical facts are critical for Christian living and for giving godly
counsel related to spiritual warfare.

Major Fact #1: The Enemy

The scriptures make it abundantly clear
that we have a spiritual enemy. Many
Christians have been taught little about this

primary warfare fact, while others have forgotten about it.

> *"Be sober, be vigilant; because your adversary the devil walks about like a roaring lion, seeking whom he may devour"*
> (1 Peter 5:8).

> *"The thief does not come except to steal, and to kill, and to destroy"* (John 10:10a).

> *"Put on the whole armor of God, that you may be able to stand against the wiles of the devil. For we do not wrestle against flesh and blood, but against principalities, against powers, against the rulers of the darkness of this age, against spiritual hosts of wickedness in the heavenly places"*
> (Ephesians 6:11-12).

Stalking our trail day after day is a spiritual foe who wants to ravage our lives, as an enraged lion would do. His only desires are to rip us off, to wipe us out, and to tear us down. This is why time and again life can seem to be a lethal wrestling match.

Consequently, although the battle may involve people, our struggle is not primarily against other people. Rather, our struggle is against *"principalities, powers, rulers of the darkness of this age, spiritual hosts of wickedness in the heavenly places"* that the enemy has available for his use. These are demonic, fallen angels who can complicate our circum-

258

stances, interfere with our relationships, and hassle our minds.

The Enemy's Broad Influence

The scriptures bear witness to the startling extent of the enemy's influence.

"We know that we are of God, and the whole world lies under the sway of the wicked one" (1 John 5:19).

"But even if our gospel is veiled, it is veiled to those who are perishing, whose minds the god of this age has blinded, who do not believe, lest the light of the gospel of the glory of Christ, who is the image of God, should shine on them" (2 Corinthians 4:3-4).

The influence of our spiritual foe is felt throughout the entire world. As the "de facto god of this age," he is blinding all those who will not believe in the true, eternal God. Consequently, in the lives of all the unsaved, as well as in all of their systems, the evil one is exercising persuasion and exerting pressure. This means that his controlling input is present in all of the systems of this world: in the educational systems, in the economic systems, in the political systems, in the religious systems, and, yes, also in the counseling systems.

The Enemy's Avenues of Enticement

As our ruthless adversary attempts to

impose his will upon the family of man, he takes particular advantage of three avenues of earthly enticement.

> *"For all that is in the world, the lust of the flesh and the lust of the eyes and the boastful pride of life, is not from the Father, but is from the world"* (1 John 2:16, NASB).

The *"lust of the flesh"* includes the natural human needs and desires, like food and clothing and sexual relationships. However, through the enemy's influence, these natural drives become distorted or perverted. The need for food can become an enticement into gluttony or a dreaded fear of gaining weight. The need for clothing can be twisted into a preoccupation with fashion or a compulsion to look better than others. The need for sexual relationship can be corrupted into fornication, adultery, homosexuality, or pornography.

The *"lust of the eyes"* includes the natural interest to see and learn and know. However, through the devil's deceiving activities, man does not see the wisdom of God in the creation around him. Instead, this desire to know becomes a striving after human intellectualism or a vain speculation in humanistic theories or a bizarre quest for cosmic consciousness.

The *"boastful pride of life"* is related to man's natural desire to find something in life that is valid and worthy, something in which he can brag and glory. However, instead of glorying in the God who made him and is willing to redeem him, man yields to the enemy's temptations to counterfeit exaltations like national pride or ethnic supremacy or self-esteem.

An Imaginary Tale of Pride and Self-Esteem

In the middle of the Twentieth Century, the church of the Lord Jesus was making significant spiritual progress. Fully aware of this threat to the forces of darkness, the devil convened a Board Meeting of his principalities and powers. Upon hearing a progress report on the church they were all appropriately troubled. They began to devise new strategies by which they might undermine the work of God among and through His people. One demonic ruler suggested that they try to get the Lord's army heavily engaged in matters of personal pride. Many others around the table scoffed excessively, reminding the rest that God's people had clearly been told that pride was totally unacceptable to the Lord.

One demonic scholar even cited multiple biblical passages to demonstrate the seeming futility of this strategy of pride.

> *"These six things the LORD hates, yes, seven are an abomination to Him: A proud look, a lying tongue . . . ."* (Proverbs 6:16-17).

> *"Everyone who is proud in heart is an*

abomination to the LORD; though they join forces, none will go unpunished" (Proverbs 16:5).

*"**Pride** goes before destruction, and a haughty spirit before a fall"* (Proverbs 16:18).

*"A man's **pride** will bring him low, but the humble in spirit will retain honor"* (Proverbs 29:23).

*"The Lord God has sworn by Himself, the LORD God of hosts says: 'I abhor the **pride** of Jacob' "* (Amos 6:8).

*"For the day of the LORD of hosts shall come upon everything **proud** and lofty, upon everything lifted up, and it shall be brought low"* (Isaiah 2:12).

*"He has shown strength with His arm; he has scattered the **proud** in the imagination of their hearts"* (Luke 1:51).

*"But He gives more grace. Therefore He says: 'God resists the **proud**, but gives grace to the humble' "* (James 4:6).

This theologically-inclined demon then assured his colleagues that enticement to pride would be ineffective. As a deceitful tactic, it was much too blatant. He insisted that hardly any believers would fall for such an obvious scheme.

However, another demonic leader urged further

consideration of the pride maneuver. He was certain that it would work, if they could only find a more acceptable, clinical euphemism to substitute for the term pride. "I know; let's call it self-esteem," one clever tactician suggested enthusiastically. The incredulous response by a majority of those present almost erupted in unison. "Do you really think that they will go for that terminology?!"

Now, at the end of the Twentieth Century, troubled and discouraged believers in Jesus Christ generally accept the popular, authoritative pronouncement coming from so many churches - - that low self-esteem is at the root of most of their problems. Thus, counselors and teachers and preachers urge people to be about the business of raising their low self-esteem. Meanwhile, demonic strategists gleefully hold their breath, hoping no church leader will unwittingly expose this demonic plot by saying to some discouraged seeker, "Now, let's see if we can help you raise the level of your boastful pride of life."

Major Fact #2: Christ's Victory

Although it is true that we are in a spiritual battle, the victory has already been won by the Lord Jesus Christ. This is the second major biblical fact concerning spiritual warfare. The enemy will not cease his fighting until he is initially bound in the bottomless pit, and then is eventually thrown into the lake of fire (see Revelation 20:1-2 and 10). Nonetheless, he has been defeated by Jesus and cannot win the battle.

Victory over Death and the Devil

Hebrews 2:14-15 describes one aspect of that victory:

> *"Inasmuch then as the children have partaken of flesh and blood, He Himself likewise shared in the same, that through death He might destroy him who had the power of death, that is, the devil, and release those who through fear of death were all their lifetime subject to bondage."*

One devastating work that Jesus has accomplished against our enemy is that He has taken away the fear of death for God's people. Satan holds humanity in a bondage of fear concerning death. Jesus has dealt with that fear of ours by coming to earth as a man and dying in our place upon the cross. Now, because He died and rose again on our behalf, we need not be afraid of death. We have life eternal in Christ, so the fear of death has lost its grip on us. This is a destructive blow that Jesus has dealt to the devil.

Victory over Demonic Forces

Colossians 2:13-15 explains another aspect of Christ's mighty victory at the cross:

> *"And you, being dead in your trespasses and the uncircumcision of your flesh, He has made alive together with Him, having*

forgiven you all trespasses, having wiped out the handwriting of requirements that was against us, which was contrary to us. And He has taken it out of the way, having nailed it to the cross. Having disarmed principalities and powers, He made a public spectacle of them, triumphing over them in it."

Because Jesus was raised from the dead, we who believe in Him were made alive with Him. Additionally, all of our failures under the law of God were canceled out, forgiven, nailed to the cross. Concurrently, the demonic cohorts of Satan were disarmed and openly defeated before all of the angelic hosts. Thereafter, every person who would depend upon this triumphant work of Christ need no longer languish in the condemnation and spiritual deadness that demonic agents love to perpetrate upon guilty sinners.

Victory over the World

In John 16:33, we are given another aspect of Christ's victory:

"These things I have spoken to you, that in Me you may have peace. In the world you will have tribulation; but be of good cheer, I have overcome the world."

One unpopular certainty of life is that we will all face difficulties and problems in this world. Yet, this truth need not discourage us. We who believe in Christ can live with a triumphant and cheerful peace, knowing that Jesus was victorious over the world. As we live in dependence upon the Lord, we need not fear what the world can bring against us. Jesus Christ, the victor over the world, is able to sustain us as we walk in this world.

A Comprehensive Victory

When we considered Romans 5 through 8 earlier in our studies, we rejoiced in the victory proclaimed therein over sin and self. When coupled with the passages that we have been examining here, the scriptures declare a comprehensive spiritual victory over the world, the flesh, the devil, sin, and self. The Lord Jesus Christ secured for His people an eternal spiritual victory over every aspect of defeat they would ever face. Our awareness of His majestic conquest, as well as our confidence in it, will determine whether or not we experience its benefits in our daily lives.

Major Fact #3: Standing in Christ's Victory

The first major fact concerning spiritual warfare is that we have an enemy, so we live on a battlefield every day. The second major fact is that Christ has provided a comprehensive spiritual victory, so we do not have to stagger about in defeat. The third major fact pertains to how we enter into that victory in a personal and practical way. Ephesians 6:10-14 contains the insight needed here:

> *"Finally, my brethren, be strong in the Lord and in the power of His might. Put on the whole armor of God, that you may be able to **stand against** the wiles of the devil. For we do not wrestle against flesh and blood, but against principalities, against powers, against the rulers of the darkness of this age, against spiritual hosts of wickedness in the heavenly places. Therefore take up the whole armor of God, that you may be able to **withstand** in the evil day, and having done all, to **stand**. **Stand** therefore, having girded your waist with truth, having put on the breastplate of righteousness."*

Basically, this classic biblical passage on spiritual warfare calls upon us to **stand** in the victory that Christ has secured. The strength for walking in victory is the strength of the Lord. The protection for remaining in victory is the armor of the Lord. God has given us truth, righteousness, the gospel, faith, salvation, and His word.

We are to prayerfully depend upon these provisions of the Lord and thereby stand victoriously. Verse 13 calls to us *"to stand."* Verse 14 adds *"stand, therefore."* Verse 10 spoke of our being able *"to stand against"* the clever tricks of our foe. Verse 13 adds similar language about us being able *"to withstand"* (literally, "stand with resistance") in times of evil attack. The Lord Jesus Christ has obtained a total triumph for His people. We are called to stand in that eternal conquest.

Such standing includes knowing and relying upon the position, victory, and resources that are ours in Christ. This victorious standing also gives full attention to what our divine Commander has to say through His word, instead of listening to the lies of the enemy or to the doubts of onlookers.

Such standing includes putting our confidence in our heavenly Conqueror, rather than in ourselves or in preferable circumstances. This triumphant standing in a world of warfare involves availability for service on the battlefield, instead of seeking after a life of ease and isolation. Proper standing would include being alert and sober and ready to engage in the battle for the souls of men and the glory of God. This Ephesians 6 type of standing would not have room for shock and amazement when the fighting waxes hot and heavy, since we accept God's word about the reality and the intensity of the warfare.

More than Conquerors

Standing in Christ's victory also includes believing that Christians are *"more than conquerors."*

*"Yet in all these things we are **more than
conquerors** through Him who loved us"*
(Romans 8:37).

Believers in Jesus Christ are not hoping
to achieve a barely perceptible win in the
last moments of a struggling and striving life.
Rather, we are learning how to face each day
by faith, knowing we already have a mighty
and monumental triumph that is ours through
Christ.

This great victory is not ours on the basis
of what we can accomplish. It is ours through
the work of the the one *"who loved us"*
enough to do what was necessary to obtain
the victory for us. Also, enjoying that triumph
does not await the removal of every unpleasant circumstance. Quite the contrary, *"in all
these things"* we are more than victorious.

*"Who shall separate us from the love of
Christ? Shall tribulation, or distress, or
persecution, or famine, or nakedness, or
peril, or sword? As it is written: For Your
sake we are killed all day long; we are
accounted as sheep for the slaughter. Yet
in all these things we are more than conquerors through Him who loved us"*
(Romans 8:35-37).

Even when we are threatened by *"tribulation, distress, persecution, famine, nakedness, peril, or sword,"* we remain *"more than*

conquerors." Even while we are *"killed all day long"* and are *"accounted as sheep for the slaughter,"* we still continue to be *"more than conquerors."* We may at times doubt these truths and, therefore, not reap all of the benefits of their reality. We may periodically become overwhelmed by our situations and, consequently, forget these blessed actualities. Nevertheless, Christ's victory is comprehensively secured and constantly available.

Conclusion and Warning

In living the Christian life, as well as in ministering God's counsel to people, we need to know that we have a spiritual foe. Furthermore, we are no match for him. Battling him with our own resources always leads to tragic, but unnecessary, defeat. However, the battle need not be between us and him. We are not to be fighting him in hand to hand combat. Remember: ***"The battle is the Lord's"*** (1 Samuel 17:47). Rightly viewed, the battle can be left between Jesus and our enemy. When this is the case, the enemy is no match for the Lord. Jesus has triumphed, and we can **stand** in **His** victory.

Let's also be alert to the tempting and distracting mentality of hunting down the devil. Some religious television can lead us to think that spiritual victory comes from baiting and haranguing the enemy. Boasts are made that

"We are going to get the devil mad tonight" or "We are going to send the devil on the run before we are finished with this program." Even good folks in good churches can get caught up in a type of warfare that seems to depend upon the vocal chords. Victory can sound like it all hinges upon how many loud and intimidating things one can shout at the enemy. This puts the focus on the wrong person. Our attention should not be upon the enemy, who has already been given defeat. It should be upon the Lord Jesus Christ who has **already won the victory.**

If we increasingly see the **triumphant work of Christ in the cross and the resurrection,** we will be less and less interested in whether the devil is mad or glad, trying to advance or considering a retreat. Rather, we will want to hear again and again that **Jesus has won the battle,** and that **we can stand** fearlessly and fruitfully and expectantly in **His comprehensive victory.**

May we be those who are learning of these realities, walking more and more in them, and then sharing them with struggling or hungry pilgrims.

Summary of Section Four on Foundational Truths

Every biblical subject matter raised in this book gives indication of why God's counsel is far superior to man's counsel. Yet, in these issues concerning **Foundational Truths**, the majesty of God's resources stands out in the clearest fashion. These truths were considered under four categories: identification with Christ, who we are in Christ, the renewing of the mind, and spiritual warfare. Herein we saw what the Lord alone provides to transform lives and make them whole.

The **identification truths** of Romans 5 through 8 reveal the cause of mankind's problems, as well as the remedies that God offers. All of man's problems are related to our beginning relationship with Adam. All of God's solutions are found in our new relationship with Jesus Christ. For everyone who has been united with the Lord Jesus through faith in Him, their old life was buried with Him in His death, and a new life was given to them in His resurrection. This gives us the opportunity to live daily on the basis of the Lord sharing His life with us.

Considering **who we are in Christ** gave us insight into what characterizes this new life. We who have placed our faith in Jesus are new creatures in Christ, branches in the true vine, and complete in Him. Such glorious revelations are given to us, not for purpose of self-enhancement, but rather that we might know how to properly relate to *"Christ, who is our life"* (Colossians 3:4).

In the **renewing of the mind**, the Lord

provides the process that transforms lives. As we are living in the Word of God, learning to view all of life as God intends, the Holy Spirit is changing our lives into a demonstration of His perfect will.

As our lives are being transformed, **spiritual warfare** is our common challenge, because we have an enemy who opposes all that God wants to bring forth. Nevertheless, a comprehensive victory is available through Christ, as we learn to stand by faith in His finished work.

There is nothing available in the realm of human theories that even begins to rival such foundational truths, for in these biblical realities the Lord has *"given to us all things that pertain to life and godliness, through the knowledge of Him"* (2 Peter 1:3).

SECTION FIVE

Major Threats to Counseling God's Way

In our fifth and final section, we will look at the **two major threats** that keep the church from counseling God's way. These threats can be discerned by looking at two major errors that kept Israel from walking in the ways of the Lord long ago.

1 Corinthians 10:11-12 tells us that we who are in the Lord's church today can learn from the failures of His people down through the ages, so that we need not foolishly stumble in the same manner:

> *"Now all these things happened to them as examples, and they were written for our admonition, on whom the ends of the ages have come. Therefore let him who thinks he stands take heed lest he fall."*

Jeremiah 2:13 discloses the two transgressions that once blocked Israel from walking in the paths of the Lord:

> *"For My people have committed two evils: they have forsaken Me, the fountain of living waters, and hewn themselves cisterns - - broken cisterns that can hold no water."*

Israel's first evil was in forsaking the Lord. This led to their second evil, hewing cisterns that could not hold water. Today, the church is paralleling Israel's wrongs of long ago. In the arena of counseling and personal discipling, many in the church are **forsaking our**

Wonderful Counselor. This is also leading to another dreadful evil, **turning to worldly counsel**. **Forsaking our Wonderful Counselor** and **turning to worldly counsel** are the two major threats that persistently interfere with the church counseling God's way.

"For My people have . . . forsaken Me,
the fountain of living waters"
— Jeremiah 2:13a

Chapter 16
Forsaking Our
Wonderful Counselor

The **main threat** to counseling God's way
among the body of Christ is not something
outside of the church. The main threat is not
the psychological theories of the world. The
major threat is that the church in many ways is
forsaking the Lord as her Wonderful Counselor.

At the beginning of our studies, we read
in Isaiah 9:6 that one of Christ's titles would
be Wonderful Counselor. Colossians 2:3 told
us that He is a counselor so wonderful that in
Him all the treasures of wisdom and knowledge are hidden. Everything needed for us to
live a life pleasing to God is found in the Lord
Jesus Christ, revealed through His word. By
His Spirit and His resources we can become

what He wants us to be for time and eternity

However, the church often forsakes the Lord by neglecting His word or disregarding His resources. Consequently, the church is left open to deception. This is very much like what happened to Israel in the days of Jeremiah: *"For My people have . . . forsaken Me, the fountain of living waters"* (Jeremiah 2:13a).

Forsaking the Lord

For Israel, God was constantly available as the *"fountain of living waters,"* to be their ever-flowing supply of spiritual reality and vitality. Tragically, they turned away from Him. God did not seem to them to be enough to satisfy the interests and cravings of their hearts. Such apostasy for Israel (also called Jeshurun) was prophesied in a song that God gave to Moses in Deuteronomy 32:15-18:

> *"But Jeshurun grew fat and kicked; you grew fat, you grew thick, you are covered with fat; then he forsook God who made him, and scornfully esteemed the Rock of his salvation. They provoked Him to jealousy with foreign gods; with abominations they provoked Him to anger. They sacrificed to demons, not to God, to gods they did not know, to new gods, new arrivals that your fathers did not fear. Of the Rock who begot you, you are unmindful, and*

have forgotten the God who fathered you."

The days were coming when Israel would grow fat with prosperity. Then, they would kick out against God in rebellion. They would forsake the true and living God who made them. They would hold in low estimation the one who was the everlasting foundation of their salvation. Idolatrous gods from the nations around them would gain their allegiance. These false gods were *"new arrivals that* (their) *fathers did not fear."* Thus, Israel would give less and less attention to the God who brought them forth from bondage to make them His people. Certainly, through it all Israel stayed very religious. Yet, God was no longer the total object of their lives, their hopes, and their activities.

This has an application to the church today. Many parts of the church world are exceedingly religious. They are involved in many of the religious activities that can be seen in the scriptures. Yet, the Lord Himself does not permeate it all. Too often, He is neither the center nor the circumference of the church's life and message. This amounts to a subtle forsaking of the Lord Jesus Christ, who has made us the people of God.

The Lord Jesus Christ is the rock of our salvation. He is the strong sustaining foundation of the divine work of rescue that God alone provides for all who believe in Jesus

Christ. The saving work of God takes us out of sin and into forgiveness, out of darkness and into light, out of the world and into His kingdom, out of Adam and into Christ, out of hopelessness and into the hope of glory.

This entire work of salvation stands upon Jesus, the rock of our salvation. Whenever we shift from Him in any way, we stumble into quicksand. Increasingly, the counseling ministry of the church is forsaking the divine rock, endeavoring to stand upon the treacherous sinking sand of humanistic theories. We are forsaking our Wonderful Counselor.

Forsaking God's Word

Forsaking the Lord inevitably leads to a forsaking of His word. 2 Chronicles 12:1 documents this disastrous development in the history of Israel:

> *"Now it came to pass, when Rehoboam had established the kingdom and had strengthened himself, that he forsook the law of the LORD, and all Israel along with him."*

The new king, Rehoboam, faced many challenges after the death of Solomon. When Rehoboam was able to establish his kingdom and strengthen his position, he forsook the word of God. Sadly, but perhaps not surprisingly, the people followed along with him.

As with Israel then, the American church

now believes that she is strong and established. We have impressive religious organizations, substantial financial treasuries, and spectacular cathedrals. We have leaders with multiple theological degrees. Some even have certifications of psychological counseling expertise from authoritative governmental agencies or prestigious worldly institutions or even from highly respected evangelical seminaries. Also, like Israel of old, many in the the church are now forsaking the word of God.

The church world is losing her confidence in the scriptures. It appears that fewer and fewer pastors are looking to God's Word as fully inspired, fully authoritative, and fully sufficient. It is amazing how notably good pastors are now quick to supplement God's word with wisdom from the world. Almost anything that purports to help people get out of a circumstantial bind or to assist their church to become a thriving religious organization will be integrated into the teaching and counseling message. This sad phenomenon is producing many church leaders who are modern day examples of the pitfalls exposed in Proverbs 28:4:

> *"Those who forsake the law praise the wicked, but such as keep the law contend with them."*

This proverb brings a sobering warning to the family of God. Believers who lose their commitment to, or confidence in, God's word will laud the godless who reject God's word. On the other hand, believers who adhere faithfully to God's word will contend with the godless who contradict God's word.

Thus in many churches today, leaders who deny in practice the sufficiency of the scriptures are very excited about psychological theory. They accept it. They commend it. They integrate it into their message and their ministry. Conversely, those leaders who are convinced of the total sufficiency of the scriptures are willing to engage in strong admonitions against any mixing of the polluted streams of humanistic theories with the pure water of the word. They want to resist the intrusion of man's wisdom into the life of God's people. They want to expose such matters. They want to protect the people of God from this deadly threat.

This battle comes down to the view we have of the word of God. Is the Bible the message of the living God Himself speaking to us? Is it His authoritative word? Is it fully sufficient to develop the true knowledge of God in our lives, thereby supplying all that we need for life and godliness? If we believe these truths about God's word, we will stand against any attempts to supplement His perfect message of deliverance, wholeness, liberty, righteousness, godliness, discipleship, and counsel.

Hearing, But Not Doing

In churches that still teach God's word, there is yet another more subtle aspect of forsaking the word of the Lord. It involves hearing the word, but not being interested in living it. James 1:21-22 speaks of this danger:

> *"Therefore lay aside all filthiness and overflow of wickedness, and receive with meekness the implanted word, which is able to save your souls. But be doers of the word, and not hearers only, deceiving yourselves."*

Here is the way that we are to come to the word of God. We are to renounce anything that is spiritually defiled or has to do with the abounding evil all around us. This would include the life we had before Christ and all the ways of fallen humanity. Then, we are to humbly allow God to plant the seed of His word into the soil of our hearts.

The reason we must receive God's word in this manner is that it alone is able to save our souls. The word of God has a divine capability to do what man's theories could never accomplish. The word of the Lord can rescue us from what destroys lives and can make us what God wants us to be. This is why it is so tragic to shift our focus and hope into any other direction. This is why it is futile to attempt to blend human speculations with God's word. Only the word of God can save our souls. May we humbly receive it.

This meek receptivity of the word includes a desire to have our lives transformed by all that God has said to us. We are to walk in the light of His truth, having our values and goals and directions in life determined by God's word. What the Bible declares is what we are to walk in and become. We are to live by the truth it proclaims.

In churches and homes and Bible colleges and seminaries, where the word of God has been read and considered in recent decades, the scriptures themselves have been proclaiming the essential realities of godly counseling ministry. In such settings, people have been exposed to the truths that have been stressed throughout this book.

Whenever Isaiah 9:6 was read, people heard God say that the Lord Himself is our Wonderful Counselor. Whenever Colossians 2:3 was read, people heard God say that all the treasures of wisdom and knowledge are hidden in our Wonderful Counselor. Whenever Psalm 19:7-8 and 119:24 were read, people heard God say that He wants to use His pure and sufficient word as His means of bringing His counsel to us. Whenever John 14:16 and 16:13 were read, people heard God say that His Spirit must be fully involved in counseling God's way. Whenever Romans 5 through 8 were read, people heard God say that He provided us with life-giving and life-changing foundational truths that work in comprehensive ways to transform our lives.

The Lord intends for us to live by these heavenly proclamations and provisions. We are not only to meekly receive these implanted words, but we are also to be giving our lives to them every day. We are to be living by these truths, not merely listening to them. Tragically, although countless numbers of believers and church leaders have heard these words that describe counseling from God's perspective, far too few have been doing them.

Consequently, in this unacceptable approach to the word of God, an approach of hearing and not doing, multitudes have been *"deceiving* (them)*selves."* Such a path of personal deception plays right into the hands of the devil himself, who delights in using deception to get us walking away from the paths of the Lord.

Crafty Deception by the Enemy

In 2 Corinthians 11:3, the Apostle Paul expressed a serious apprehension regarding deception inside the church of the Lord Jesus Christ. Many Christians and church leaders today share a similar concern.

> *"But I fear, lest somehow, as the serpent deceived Eve by his craftiness, so your minds may be corrupted* (or, led astray)

*from the **simplicity** that is in Christ."*

The Apostle Paul was concerned that some in the church might drift away from *"the simplicity that is in Christ."* The message of the word of God is astoundingly simple. Everything that everyone needs for time and eternity is found in the Lord Jesus Christ. This is true whether we are considering forgiveness of sins, developing a godly life, finding purpose in life, or the counseling we ultimately need throughout all of life. Jesus Christ is to be *"all in all"* (Colossians 3:11) to His people.

The enemy of our souls wants to lead us away from this *"simplicity that is in Christ."* The tactic that he uses is crafty deception, just as he did with Eve. The devil came into the garden and began to reason with Eve, bringing into question the word of the Lord. Satan did not offer himself and his ways as a blatant substitute for God and His ways. Rather, by cunning enticement he seduced Eve to lose confidence in the simple path that God had provided for man.

In recent decades, the devil has cleverly used the intriguing field of psychology to entice God's people to forsake the Lord as our Wonderful Counselor. It may be true that the psychological theories of man are the most crafty tactic the enemy has ever used against mankind in general and the Lord's church in particular.

These theories have an appearance of scientific certainty. They seem to offer insightful and profound answers for the struggles and problems of man. They come from intellectual geniuses holding various degrees of higher learning. When compared with the *"the simplicity that is in Christ,"* these complicated speculations give the impression that we must integrate them into our thinking and ministering. To set aside such impressive possibilities would appear to be shortsighted, narrow-minded, or unsophisticated. How clever of our enemy, who comes only to rob, kill, and destroy, to provide impotent theories that promise life and wholeness, but instead deliver death and bondage.

Deception in the Church Prophesied

Through these attractive theories, the enemy is leading many believers astray from the simple and sufficient truths found in the Lord Jesus Christ. God forewarned us in His word that such would be happening in the last days.

> *"Now the Spirit expressly says that in latter times some will depart from the faith, giving heed to deceiving spirits and doctrines of demons"* (1 Timothy 4:1).

"The faith" is the message of the God's word in which we are to place our faith and

confidence. The Holy Spirit says here in explicit terms that the days were coming when some in the church would drift away from the message of God's word. People would shift their allegiance from the scriptures. This process of forsaking what God has said would involve paying attention to what deceiving demonic spirits would have to say.

This is an extremely sobering prophecy when we consider the basic source of psychological theories. They come from the world's great thinkers, not from the apostles and prophets of old or from the pastors and biblical theologians of today. The entire framework of psychological theory came from those who were *"under the sway of the wicked one"* (1 John 5:19). Their doctrines are truly, even if inadvertently, *"doctrines of demons."*

This does not mean that every Christian in psychological therapy is under the control of demonic influence. This does not imply that every Christian who is a psychologist or a psychiatrist is sold out to the devil. Neither does it say that every Christian teacher, counselor, Bible college, or seminary that is attempting to integrate psychological theory into Christian ministry is apostate. There are many dear people of God who have been caught up in some aspects of psychological training.

Nonetheless, such involvement with these worldly theories introduces spiritually destructive concepts into lives, homes, churches, biblical training centers, and co-called Christian counseling clinics. Therefore, it amounts to a grievous forsaking of our Wonderful Counselor, by straying from *"the simplicity that is in Christ."*

Simple, but not Simplistic

Many people seem to wrongly think that *"the simplicity that is in Christ"* infers that the message of Christ is simplistic, that is, non-substantial or insufficient. Nothing could be further from actuality. The *"simplicity that is in Christ"* centers around the uncomplicated fact that all man needs and all God has for man is found in Christ (which would include His written revelation, the Bible).

That same simplicity includes the additional fact that all of God's provisions in Christ are available to man through a relationship of faith: *"The just shall live by faith"* (Romans 1:17). These truths are simple enough for a child to understand and benefit from them. On the other hand, the depths of the realities of God's grace that are found in Christ are such that they could never be exhaustively comprehended by even the greatest redeemed minds among His children.

The resources contained within *"the simplicity that is in Christ"* are beyond measure. Yet, they can be known in our own personal experience by believing and receiving.

> *"Oh, the depth of the riches both of the wisdom and knowledge of God! How unsearchable are His judgments and His ways past finding out!"* (Romans 11:33).

> *"But as it is written: Eye has not seen, nor ear heard, nor have entered into the heart of man the things which God has prepared for those who love Him. But God has revealed them to us through His Spirit. For the Spirit searches all things, yes, the deep things of God"* (1 Corinthians 2:9-10).

> *"To me, who am less than the least of all the saints, this grace was given, that I should preach among the Gentiles the unsearchable riches of Christ"* (Ephesians 3:8).

> *". . . that in the ages to come He might show the exceeding riches of His grace in His kindness toward us in Christ Jesus"* (Ephesians 2:7).

> *". . . that He would grant you, according to the riches of His glory, to be strengthened with might through His Spirit in the inner man"* (Ephesians 3:16).

> *". . . to know the love of Christ which passes knowledge; that you may be filled with all the fullness of God"* (Ephesians 3:19).

"And the Word became flesh and dwelt among us, and we beheld His glory, the glory as of the only begotten from the Father, full of grace and truth. And of His fullness we have all received, and grace upon grace" (John 1:14, 16, NASB).

Note some of the compelling phrases in scripture that speak of the substantial spiritual riches that are available in Christ: *"Oh, the depth of the riches . . . the deep things of God . . . the unsearchable riches of Christ . . . the exceeding riches of His grace . . . the riches of His glory . . . the fullness of God . . . full of grace and truth."*

These are heavenly realities that we could never discover or comprehend on our own. *"How unsearchable are His judgments and His ways past finding out!" "Eye has not seen, nor ear heard, nor have entered into the heart of man the things which God has prepared for those who love Him."*

Nevertheless, God has His ways of bringing these glorious blessings into our lives. *"But God has revealed them to us through His Spirit." "And the Word became flesh and dwelt among us, and we beheld His glory, the glory as of the only begotten from the Father, full of grace and truth. And of His fullness we have all received, and grace upon grace."* Jesus Christ came to earth to provide all of these riches for us. The Holy Spirit unfolds these treasures unto

293

us (the people of God) - - and through us to all who will hear and believe and receive.

To think that *"the simplicity that is in Christ"* is simplistic, that is, non-substantial or insufficient, amounts to a subtle but deadly form of forsaking our Wonderful Counselor

Conclusion

We must not forsake Jesus as our Wonderful Counselor, because this is the number one major threat to counseling God's way. Forgiveness, cleansing, and eternal life are found in Christ alone. Only He can reclaim, restore, and rebuild lives. He is the only One who can provide abundant life and wholeness of life and transformation of life. Jesus alone brings spiritual freedom, spiritual growth, and spiritual victory.

Whenever we doubt that He is sufficient, we have to some degree forsaken Him by limiting all that He is intended to be in our lives. Furthermore, yielding to this primary threat always leads to **the corollary threat: turning to worldly counsel.** This second threat will be examined extensively in the next chapter.

"For My people have . . . hewn themselves cisterns, broken cisterns that can hold no water."
— Jeremiah 2:13b

Chapter 17
Turning to Worldly Counsel

Turning to worldly counsel is the **second** of the two major threats to counseling God's way in the church. This second threat is **an inevitable consequence** of yielding to the **first** threat, which is **forsaking our Wonderful Counselor.** Those who consider that the Lord Jesus Christ and His word are not sufficient for people's counseling needs will end up searching for supplementary answers in the psychological systems of the world. This is like what Israel did when they forsook the Lord.

Broken Cisterns

When Israel forsook the Lord as her fountain of living waters, she looked for ways to collect some kind of "substitute water" by which to live.

> *"For My people have . . . hewn themselves cisterns, broken cisterns that can hold no water"* (Jeremiah 2:13b).

In forsaking the Lord, Israel became vulnerable to the temptations of the worldly, idolatrous religious systems all around them. As the people of the true and living God began to turn to these false gods, they were virtually digging cisterns that would prove to be flawed. These religious cisterns could not actually contain the water that was needed for living life God's way.

This is what the church of the Lord Jesus Christ is doing today by seeking out the humanistic input of the world's psychological theories. We are hewing for ourselves man-made systems of sustenance, refreshment, and supply. Can we not see that if God is not the source, the systems of thought are going to be flawed and defective? They will be full of holes. The systems will not hold water. They will not provide counseling God's way.

Strange Doctrines

Those in the church world who pass on these flawed psychological systems of man to the people of God are actually involved in teaching strange doctrines. God has given us strong warnings against such a practice.

> *"As I urged you upon my departure from Macedonia, remain on at Ephesus, in order that you may instruct certain men not to teach strange doctrines, nor to pay attention to myths and endless genealogies, which give rise to mere speculation rather than furthering the administration of God which is by faith"* (1 Timothy 1:3-4, NASB).

From the early days of the church, various people needed to be told not to teach *"strange doctrines."* Such unacceptable doctrines would include all teaching that is foreign to the word of God. This issue was urgent to the Apostle Paul. He beseeched Timothy to stay in Ephesus to confront this danger. We must give this matter the same priority in our lives, ministries, and churches.

Strange doctrines are clearly evident today in the counseling perspectives of many churches. The leaders, teachers, and counselors of these churches earnestly need to be instructed not to teach their unbiblical counseling approaches. If any tenet of counseling cannot be found in the word of God, it is a strange doctrine that is to be exposed and rejected.

Myths and Speculations

These words from 1 Timothy indicate that myth and speculation are related to the teaching of strange doctrines. Superstitions, fables, fantasies, opinions, conjectures, and wild presuppositions abound in the darkened minds of unredeemed humanity. Thus, it is not surprising that myth and speculation characterize the psychological counseling systems of man. Although the Lord has warned us not to pay attention to such worldly surmising, many Christians eagerly give and receive counsel based upon such unfounded human thinking.

The Myth of Psychoanalysis

Psychoanalysis is one myth that many in the church world view as a valid, even necessary, counseling technique. This procedure is used in many varying approaches by trained professionals and self-taught practitioners alike. Basically, in this technique, the counselor encourages the counselee to undertake an introspective evaluation of thoughts, feelings, motivations, and attitudes. Then, as the inner responses to issues, individuals, and events are disclosed, the counselor seeks explanations and understandings by searching that person's history of relationships and experiences.

There is another popular "Umbrella Cliché" that encourages and attempts to justify such an approach to counseling.

Man's Inward and Backward Directions

In psychoanalytical counseling, the person seeking help is directed inward and backward, on the assumption that people's lives can be explained by the sum total of their experiences from birth to the present. Such speculation cannot be proven concerning humanity in general. Furthermore, it is certainly not applicable to believers in the Lord Jesus Christ.

The evaluation and explanation of our lives, as well as the resources for needed change, are all found in our relationship to Christ. Who He is, what He has done, what He offers to us, and what He can do in and through us is where we find our insight and hope and life itself. In many ways, attempting to help Christians by digging into their past is like trying to find life by digging in a graveyard.

God's Forward and Upward Directions

These humanistic directions of inward and backward are filled with deadly danger, because they are the opposite directions of the counsel of God. In the kingdom of heaven,

lives are transformed and developed by looking **forward** and **upward**.

> *"Not that I have already attained, or am*
> *already perfected; but I press on, that I*
> *may lay hold of that for which Christ Jesus*
> *has also laid hold of me. Brethren, I do*
> *not count myself to have apprehended;*
> *but one thing I do, forgetting those things*
> *which are behind and reaching **forward***
> *to those things which are ahead, I press*
> *toward the goal for the prize of the*
> ***upward** call of God in Christ Jesus"*
> (Philippians 3:12-14).

After many years of Christian growth and
service, the Apostle Paul humbly admitted that
he had not attained the fullness of all that God
had for him when He saved his soul. However,
an introspective journey into himself and his
past were not his hope of progress. In fact,
he was laying the past aside, forgetting it.
Instead, he was pressing forward and looking
upward. He was moving forward toward the
goal of getting to know the Lord better: *"I also*
count all things loss for the excellence of the
knowledge of Christ Jesus my Lord . . . that I
may know Him" (verses 8 and 10). In doing
this, he was answering the upward, heavenly
call of the Lord to be growing in his knowing
of God.

Colossians 3:2-3 strongly emphasizes this
upward call of God:

"Set your mind on things above, not on things on the earth. For you died, and your life is hidden with Christ in God."

Believers in Jesus Christ are called to focus their attention upon things above, that is, on heavenly matters. This involves concentrating upon the Lord and His purposes and His promises and His resources. This heavenly perspective then provides meaning, hope, and fulfillment through God's love, truth, mercy, and grace.

On the other hand, Christians are not to focus their attention upon things on the earth. This would involve concentrating upon ourselves, our circumstances, our will, and our capabilities. Such an earthly perspective results in spiritual stagnation and frustration and fruitlessness because of the spiritual bankruptcy of the flesh.

The ultimate reason why we must seek heavenly things and not pursue earthly things is given in verse 3. Those who have put their faith in the Lord Jesus died on the cross with Him. The Father brought their old lives to an end at the crucifixion of His Son. The new life that is available to all followers of the Lord is *"hidden with Christ in God."* This new life is not found in self or circumstances or any other earthly resource. It is found only in Christ.

The true Christian life that God intends for us to walk in can only be developed as we daily seek the Lord Himself, finding in Him our strength, our wisdom, our hope, our everything. Walking with the Lord in these forward and upward directions allows us to increasingly experience the realities of *"Christ who is our life,"* a life wherein *"Christ is all and in all"* (Colossians 3:3, 11).

The Myth of Control by the Subconscious Mind

Control by the subconscious mind is another speculative counseling myth embraced by many in contemporary churches. This strange doctrine claims that people's lives are controlled by that which dwells in their minds beneath the level of conscious thoughts. Another popular cliché expresses this perspective.

> **UMBRELLA CLICHÉ #8:**
> **"People are controlled by issues buried within their subconscious minds, therefore they must uncover these matters, if they are going to find real help."**

It may or may not be demonstrable that this is an avenue of attack the devil can use to bind unbelievers (or even believers who are walking according to the flesh). Yet, whether this is possible or not, man's hope of victory and freedom is not in attempting to surface these supposed subconscious thoughts.

Rather, man's hope is in coming to Christ as Lord and Savior, and then learning to think and live by the thoughts of God. Such heavenly thinking is definitely possible for the children of God, since *"we have the mind of Christ"* (1 Corinthians 2:16). The Spirit of Christ dwells in His people to unfold to them through the scriptures the very mind of the Lord. Learning to think as the Lord thinks is certainly a more than sufficient resource for release from any real (or imagined) control by subconscious thoughts.

The Myths of Mental Illness and Sick Behavior

Another strange doctrine in the church world is the fable that undesirable thinking and behaving are actually mental illness and sick behavior. Today, people are told that they are suffering from the disease of alcoholism, instead of the sin of drunkenness. They are told that they are suffering from a shopping disorder, instead of the sin of covetousness. Sadly, the biblical concepts of **ungodly thinking** and **sinful behavior** are disappearing in the teaching and counseling of many church leaders. Issues of ungodliness and sinfulness are being eclipsed by a new pathological vocabulary of diseases and disorders. Consequently, God's true remedies for real problems are by-passed in place of man's counterfeit remedies for imagined problems.

Such assertions do not mean that biblical counselors are to deny **actual physiological problems** that can plague humanity. Being committed to the word of God, instead of to the psychological theories of man, does not mean one refuses to acknowledge such problems as brain diseases or genetic brain maladies. True biblical counseling is not a matter of taking erroneous Christian Science theology into the counseling arena. We are not denying that man has real physical illnesses.

The scriptures describe man as having a physical aspect to his makeup, and this physical aspect can contract diseases and can function improperly. The Bible does not forbid medical ministry to sick people. Jesus said, *"Those who are well do not need a physician, but those who are sick"* (Luke 5:31). Luke is referred to as *"the beloved physician"* (Colossians 4:14), not as some renegade believer that must leave the medical profession.

Consequently, even such matters as "chemical imbalances" are potentially valid in the physical constitution of human beings. Yet, how to measure all of these possible imbalances often eludes the best of medical technology. Furthermore, whether the imbalance is the cause or effect of wrong thinking and behaving lies within a challenging realm of uncertainty. Additionally, an unnecessary or unhealthy dependency can develop toward chemical solutions for physical (and even emotional) needs. Nevertheless, many seekers and helpers alike are inappropriately assuming that medication is an essential part of assisting most needy souls.

Ideally, godly, capable medical doctors (including those proficient in the intricacies of the physical organ of the brain) can minister to people's physical needs, while godly, mature Christians can minister to the spiritual needs. Regretfully, both the physical and non-physical needs in lives are now dealt with by a new priesthood of psychiatrists that can authorize medication for physical matters, while offering humanistic philosophical answers for the non-physical matters. This trend is increasingly usurping the roles of both the biblically-permitted medical doctor, as well as the biblically-prescribed spiritual counselor.

As stated earlier, this does not mean that people in the mental health professions can never be used of God. However, those whom the Lord is using are being used in spite of their training in speculative humanistic psychological theories, not on the basis of such training. Once again, whenever a believer working in the mental health field lays aside his worldly philosophical training and directs needy people toward the Lord and His resources, God will use that person in a wonderful way.

The Bible points needy people toward the Lord. No other path will ever meet their deepest needs. It is the Lord alone who can fully validate medical options, provide the necessary sustaining strength, or produce desired wholeness. Ultimately, whether human instruments are involved or not, we should all encourage one another to adopt David's confession of the Lord as his hope and sufficiency.

> *"The LORD is my rock and my fortress and my deliverer; My God, my strength, in whom I will trust; My shield and the horn of my salvation, my stronghold"* (Psalm 18:2).

> *"My soul, wait silently for God alone, For my expectation is from Him. He only is my rock and my salvation; He is my defense; I shall not be moved. In God is my salvation and my glory; The rock of my strength, And my refuge, is in God. Trust in Him at all times, you people; Pour out your heart before Him; God is a refuge for us"* (Psalm 62:5-9).

The Self-Love Myth

One popular counseling delusion with enormous impact in the church world is the self-love myth. This strange doctrine was developed by secular psychological theoreticians like Carl Rogers, Abraham Maslow, Alfred Adler, William James, and Eric Fromm. This theory claims that people must learn to love themselves, if they are to have effective and fulfilled lives.

Severe torturing of the word of God has introduced this anti-biblical assertion into the mainstream of modern church teaching and counseling. I was first exposed to this particular adulterating of scripture in 1967, while serving as a Youth Pastor in Southern California. Our church had sent our high school group to a Youth Camp at one of the largest and most respected Christian Conference Centers in the state. The guest speaker was from a major evangelical seminary. The text for his lamentable, yet unforgettable, message was from the gospel of Matthew.

> *"Then one of them, a lawyer, asked Him a question, testing Him, and saying, 'Teacher, which is the great commandment in the law?' Jesus said to him, 'You shall love the Lord your God with all your heart, with all your soul, and with all your mind. This is the first and great commandment. And the second is like it: You shall love your neighbor as yourself. On these two commandments hang all the Law and the Prophets' "* (Matthew 22:35-40).

After this passage from the word of God

was read, the speaker made an enticing fleshly statement, which opened the door to a subtle and deceitful exposition of the scriptures. His statement was: "People generally do not really love themselves as they should." "Therefore," he added, "this scripture is instructing us to be about the business of learning to love ourselves more and more in the way that we should." He further stated, "Eventually, we will be able to love others as we are learning to properly love ourselves." He later concluded: "Ultimately, we will even be able to get on with the higher matter of loving God."

Today, the messages of best-selling religious books, high-rating Christian radio broadcasts, and well-attended evangelical churches indicate that this erroneous self-love message prevails among the churches.

Many would question why this teaching should ever be challenged. Well, on the one hand, it distorts the overall perspective of the scriptures that every believer is to have toward self and toward God. Such matters have been dealt with in various places throughout this book (see particularly Chapters 2 and 10). On the other hand, this message radically violates the very passage from which this self-love myth is taught.

Three Significant Errors

From just within the confines of this

Matthew 22:35-40 passage, there are three significant errors in this self-love exposition. First, Jesus said that there are two commandments in this message that He was giving, not three. Repeatedly, we are warned in the word of God not to add to it or to take away from it (see Deuteronomy 4:2 and 12:32; Proverbs 30:5-6; and Revelation 22:18-19). This is a very serious issue in itself. Jesus did not command us to go and learn to love ourselves. Such a fable comes from adding to the word of God. When Jesus tells us to *"love your neighbor as yourself,"* He is commanding us to give the loving attention to others that all of us have naturally and selfishly been giving to ourselves.

Second, Jesus said that everything in the scriptures hangs upon these two commandments. Everything in the word of God is about loving God or loving others. There is nothing left in the word of God that relates to this imaginary third commandment to be learning to love ourselves.

Third, and most critical of all, this false teaching reverses the priority that Jesus is giving in these two commandments. Jesus' teaching here is designed to send people out into life concentrating upon learning to love God with all of their being. Loving God *"is the first and great commandment."* Contrariwise, when this self-love myth is wrongfully forced upon this teaching of Jesus, people are sent forth to concentrate upon learning to love themselves?!? Such an outcome is diametrically opposed to what Jesus was intending to instill in people's lives.

Other Popular Counseling Myths

There are many other popular counseling myths that have come into the life and ministry of churches and religious organizations these days. Among them are the intriguing arenas of **temperament analysis** and **birth order.**

Understanding one's own **temperament** is now viewed by some as a key to maximizing development as a person. Some Christians have become more interested in examining their own temperament types than in becoming more familiar with the distinctives of the nature of Jesus. Without the Lord being present and active in our lives, every person on earth would display an "Adamic depraved" type of temperament.

Essentially, whatever temperament types other people may ascribe to us, God wants to transform our temperaments more and more into the image of His own beloved Son. People actually need counseling that directs them away from a focus on their own natural attributes and, instead, points them toward a greater understanding of the Lord Jesus Christ. Conformity to Christ is what the Lord desires for our lives. Such spiritual transformation is caused by the Spirit of God working in hearts that are looking into the word of God to see the glories of the character of the Son of God.

> *"But we all, with unveiled face, beholding as in a mirror the glory of the Lord, are being transformed into the same image from glory to glory, just as by the Spirit of the Lord"* (2 Corinthians 3:18).

Birth order theories are also finding unwarranted acceptance within the Christian community. In this realm of thinking, a person's place in the birth sequence is seen as establishing certain built-in attitudes and tendencies that will become a major determinative influence in his life.

Again, though theoreticians may be able to build a seemingly plausible case for such matters among the unredeemed lives of the world, such a perspective has no valid place in the thinking of the Lord's redeemed children. In our lives, the determinative elements of growing and developing properly are related to the realities that come with every new spiritual birth, not from the order of natural birth.

> *"That which is born of the flesh is flesh, and that which is born of the Spirit is spirit. Do not marvel that I said to you, 'You must be born again' "* (John 3:6-7).

"Blessed be the God and Father of our Lord Jesus Christ, who according to His abundant mercy has begotten us again to a living hope through the resurrection of Jesus Christ from the dead" (1 Peter 1:3).

"Therefore, if anyone is in Christ, he is a new creation; old things have passed away; behold, all things have become new" (2 Corinthians 5:17).

Speculation or Faith

Why is it so necessary to expose and avoid these "strange doctrines" and "myths"? It is because such unbiblical ideas *"give rise to mere speculation, rather than furthering the administration of God which is by faith"* (1 Timothy 1:4, NASB). The administration of God, His work in and with lives, takes place through faith. The Lord reclaims lives, restores lives, and rules over lives by faith, not by speculation. God touches and changes people as they put their trust in Him and His word. Speculation has to do with unreliable human conjectures and propositions and theories. Such unreliable earthbound perspectives interfere with the work that God wants to do, a work which is accomplished by faith in God and the revealed truth of His word.

"For in it the righteousness of God is revealed from faith to faith; as it is writ-

ten, 'The just shall live by faith' " (Romans
1:17).

*"But without faith it is impossible to please
Him, for he who comes to God must believe
that He is, and that He is a rewarder of
those who diligently seek Him"* (Hebrews
11:6).

*"So shall I have an answer for him who
reproaches me, For I trust in Your word"*
(Psalm 119:42).

*"Those who fear You will be glad when
they see me, Because I have hoped in Your
word"* (Psalm 119:74).

*"You are my hiding place and my shield;
I hope in Your word"* (Psalm 119:114).

Man's Wisdom, Not God's Wisdom

Another way to evaluate all of these matters pertaining to strange doctrines and myths
is to note that they are man's wisdom, not
God's wisdom. 1 Corinthians 1:18-21 reveals
how critical the distinction is between human
wisdom and divine wisdom:

*"For the message of the cross is foolishness
to those who are perishing, but to us who
are being saved it is the power of God. For
it is written: I will destroy the wisdom of
the wise, and bring to nothing the understanding of the prudent. Where is the*

313

wise? Where is the scribe? Where is the disputer of this age? Has not God made foolish the wisdom of this world? For since, in the wisdom of God, the world through wisdom did not know God, it pleased God through the foolishness of the message preached to save those who believe."

The wisdom of God to save lives through the death of His Son on a cross sounds foolish to those perishing ones who will not yield to the ways of God. Yet, that message is actually the power of God unto salvation for all who believe. God's wisdom actually makes the wisdom of man foolish, since man cannot even begin a relationship with God through all of his human wisdom. Thus, God desires to tear down and demolish this inept understanding that man puts forth from his finest speculations.

1 Corinthians 3:19-20 adds more heavenly light on this theme:

"For the wisdom of this world is foolishness with God. For it is written, 'He catches the wise in their own craftiness;' and again, 'The Lord knows the thoughts of the wise, that they are futile'."

"Foolishness" is God's estimation of the wisdom that comes from man's great thinkers. Consider the implications of this remarkable

and humbling truth. As far as God is concerned, man's most profound contemplations are marked by absurdity and senselessness and folly. Furthermore, God was always fully aware of the theories that would be generated by Freud and Jung and Adler and Maslow and all of the other humanly revered psychological geniuses: *"The Lord knows the thoughts of the wise."* Yet, notice His ultimate pronouncement upon their reasonings: *"They are futile."* This means that their reasonings are **ineffectual** and **useless** for the purposes of God in people's lives. So, why oh why, would the church of the Lord Jesus Christ ever want to integrate such bankrupt theorizing into her message and ministry?

Twelve-Step Self-Help Recovery Programs

In a discussion of the wisdom of man, one widely accepted counseling approach in the church world warrants some evaluation. This is the "Twelve-Step Self-Help Recovery Program." Many churches develop small group programs based upon these twelve steps that originated with the Alcoholics Anonymous movement. Generally, scripture is correlated to some degree with these twelve stated principles to give the program a Christian tone or emphasis. Then, hurting or needy folks are gathered together by their commonly expressed problems, such as: alcohol, fears, drugs, unwholesome relationships, and many other afflictions.

The testimonies of innumerable Christian participants give the impression that God's great blessings characteristically accompany these programs. Some involved believers tell how they came to know the Lord through such a group. Others relate how their suffering and anguish were relieved. Still others speak of renewed interest in and hunger for God. During thirty years of ministry, I have had many of these testimonies substantially and extensively validated. Nevertheless, I am concerned over the ingrained presence and contaminating influence of man's wisdom that generally accompanies the "Twelve-Step Programs."

The problem arises from the starting point of these programs. Beginning with twelve human principles, and then attempting to fit substantiating scriptures to each of them, creates a built-in earthbound bias. Furthermore, although some of these twelve steps may be easily adapted to the word of God, with others the attempt to make the principles appear biblical can end up strained, forced, or artificial. In addition, grouping people together around their common heartaches and personal shortcomings establishes a sort of mutual commiseration society. Jointly-held problems can become the fellowship focus, instead of a common relationship with the Lord Jesus

Christ.

Moreover, participants are encouraged to adopt non-biblical confessions that violate their true identity in Christ. The programs foster statements like: "I am a recovering alcoholic" or "I am a recovering sex offender." Such confessions explain identity by sin and failure, rather than by relationship to Christ. A believer who is in bondage to drunkenness is not "a recovering alcoholic." Rather, that Christian is a child of God who needs to learn to walk in the forgiveness and victory available to all who are new creatures in Christ.

How can it be that valid testimonies of spiritual fruit come from a movement significantly marred by the presence of futile human conjecturing? Well, part of the answer lies in the fact that God is not a condemnatory Pharisee. God does not require that we have a flawlessly correlated, and perfectly applied, biblical theology before He comes to our aid or does any work of mercy and grace among us. If that were the nature of our God, none of us would ever see any of His work in and through any of our lives. No one but Jesus ever had it all together theologically and spiritually.

Another part of the answer comes from the fact that some twelve-step groups embrace various spiritual realities that God blesses and uses. Some groups exercise biblical measures of truth, faith, hope, love, mercy, compassion, and humility. The Holy Spirit can certainly find some room to work in such hearts.

However, having acknowledged all of this, there is still no spiritual justification for developing and relying upon these programs that lean heavily upon the wisdom of man. We can, at the same time, give God glory and thanks for anything He does in any group or movement, while earnestly crying out that we forsake the wisdom of man, desiring to cling wholly unto the wisdom of God.

The Lord's church would gain much and lose nothing, if we traded off the "Twelve-Step Self-Help Recovery Programs" for God's irreplaceable biblical realities. Christ-centered discipleship, involving Spirit-empowered Bible study and prayer, is what transforms lives. God's pattern for recovery is to first invite people to begin following the Lord. Then, we are to gather as His followers in churches, in small groups, and in one-to-one settings, with Christ as the focus, seeking together to know Him better. Therein, God Himself restores lives into what He desires them to become.

Flesh, Not Spirit

One final manner in which we will appraise these issues involving strange doctrines and myths is to take into account that they are matters of the flesh, not of the Spirit. In this chapter, we have given attention to various counseling perspectives that are permeated with psychological theories and self-centered philosophies. The source of such systems is the flesh of man, not the Spirit of God. Jeremiah 17:5-8 depicts some of the drastic differences between these two resources:

> *"Thus says the LORD:* **Cursed** *is the man who trusts in man and makes flesh his strength, whose heart departs from the LORD. For he shall be like a shrub in the desert, and shall not see when good comes, but shall inhabit the parched places in the wilderness, in a salt land which is not inhabited.* **Blessed** *is the man who trusts in the* **LORD,** *and whose hope is the* **LORD.** *For he shall be like a tree planted by the waters, which spreads out its roots by the river, and will not fear when heat comes; but her leaf will be green, and will not be anxious in the year of drought, nor will cease from yielding fruit."*

The difference between flesh and Spirit is as radical as the difference between a cursing and a blessing. Those who put their hopes in the flesh of man, in natural human resources, are cursed. Their lives become like sparse desert bushes, never knowing true abundance of spiritual vitality. Consequently, those who trust in the flesh-conceived psychological theories of man would be partaking of this curse that is inherent to the flesh.

Conversely, those who put their hope in what the Lord can do by His Spirit are fully blessed. Their lives become like the luxuriant, verdant trees growing on the banks of a pristine, bountiful river. Such lives consistently yield abundance of fruit and dwell in spiritual tranquility even in seasons of stress and circumstantial difficulty. This is the blessing that is upon those who trust in the heavenly counseling resources of our Wonderful Counselor and His Holy Spirit through His word.

Jesus spoke of this critical contrast between the flesh and the Spirit.

> *"It is the Spirit who gives life; the flesh profits nothing"* (John 6:63).

True life, spiritual life, must come initially and continually from the presence and work of the Holy Spirit. Every child of God received eternal life when he was born again by the Spirit of God through faith in Jesus Christ. In the same way, every child of God can only grow and abound in that everlasting life by the ongoing work of the Spirit of the Lord. The fleshly resources of humanistic counseling systems can provide no life-giving or life-developing benefits in the kingdom of God. My heart aches when I see the church of Jesus Christ trying to integrate biblical truth and psychological theory, because *the flesh profits nothing.*

Galatians 3:3 brings to this discussion a

compelling question with a biblically obvious answer:

> *"Are you so foolish? Having begun in the Spirit, are you now being made perfect by the flesh?"*

We who follow the Lord began this spiritual walk by the work of the Spirit of God. The Spirit brought the message of the gospel to us through some means whereby we heard the truth about our sin and about salvation in Jesus Christ. The Holy Spirit then convicted us of the reality of our need and the reliability of Jesus as Savior. We put our trust in the Lord Jesus to save us, and we were born again by the Spirit of God from above.

We began by the Spirit. Now, are we so foolish as to think that we can grow, develop, and progress in this new life in Christ by human fleshly devices? Tragically, many within the church world who are relying upon the integration of man's psychological theories would have to respond: "Yes, we are that foolish!"

UMBRELLA CLICHÉ #9:
"You go to a body-doctor when your body is not functioning properly; so why won't you go to a mind-doctor when your mind is not functioning properly?"

This umbrella cliché is eventually raised

321

by some people when the church is being warned about the integration of psychological counseling theories. On the surface, the reasoning appears legitimate. Yet, all legitimacy vanishes when we realize that the comparison of a "body-doctor" and a "mind-doctor" is even less appropriate than comparing apples and oranges. Actually, it is like comparing apples and toxins.

As previously stated, the scriptures do not prohibit Christians from accepting "common grace" assistance from a medical doctor. On the other hand, the word of God strongly prohibits believers from accepting guidance that is based upon the philosophical speculations of a "mind-doctor." Colossians 2:8 provides such a biblical admonition:

> *"Beware lest anyone cheat you through philosophy and empty deceit, according to the tradition of men, according to the basic principles of the world, and not according to Christ."*

Followers of Christ are to be on the alert against anyone who might *"cheat you through philosophy,"* or *"take you captive through philosophy"* (NASB). Speaking of the fundamental threat to His sheep, Jesus said:

> *"The thief does not come except to steal, and to kill, and to destroy. I have come that they may have life, and that they may*

have it more abundantly" (John 10:10).

In the truth and reality that Jesus provides, there is abundant life. The enemy of men's souls, functioning as the usurping, counterfeit "god of this age," wants to keep people from entering into that fullness of life. His strategy includes propagating a polluted stream of human philosophy, vain deceits, traditions of men, and basic worldly principles that will take people captive, leading them away from the truth of God's word.

The psychological theories that are used by the "mind-doctor" are drawn from the polluted philosophical stream of human conjecture. We are to *"beware lest anyone"* influences our lives by such thinking. This category of "anyone" would include openly atheistic therapists, well-intended Christian psychological clinicians, and even popular and well-respected national church leaders. Our lives are to be guided and directed only by that which is *"according to Christ."*

Conclusion

Whenever, and to whatever degree, God's people **forsake their** Wonderful Counselor, they will eventually end up **turning to worldly counsel.** This is what happens when we diminish our allegiance to the *"fountain of living waters."* We attempt to scratch out a meager existence around *"broken cisterns that* *can hold no water.*" We are willing to settle for strange doctrines and myths.

Our attention is turned within ourselves and back into our past, instead of gazing upward into heavenly things and looking forward to see what the Lord will do next in our lives. Our desire to learn the mind of Christ is sidetracked into the futile quest to unlock our own subconscious mind. Our passion becomes loving ourselves, instead of loving the Lord with all of our being. The work of the Spirit can be quenched by carnal craving for that which satisfies the flesh. We are vulnerable to shifting our expectations from faith in God and His word to confidence in man and his latest speculations. Man's wisdom begins to have a greater appeal than God's wisdom.

In such a place of spiritual danger, the recovery support group easily displaces the Bible study discipleship group. Integrating psychology with the word of God is no longer viewed as a threat, but rather, it becomes the expectation of wholeness for us and those we desire to help. The Christian psychological clinic can appear to offer more hope than the church of the Lord Jesus Christ. The infinite, reliable riches that are ours in Christ diminish in our estimation, while the finite, unreliable novelties of human philosophy take on increasing value.

In all such tragic drifting, **we are shifting**

from a Christ-centered biblical view of life to a man-centered philosophical perspective. Lamentably, many within the church world are extensively involved in this theological departure. May we be ever alert and prayerful, earnestly seeking the Lord, so that we will not join their ranks. May we reach out to them, **speak the truth in love**, and **fervently pray** that they will fully return to the **Wonderful Counselor**.

Conclusion:
A Reformation in Counseling

The **counseling crisis** in the church world is primarily related to many Christians either misunderstanding or underestimating **the fundamental differences between biblical counseling and psychological counseling.** It would be profitable to reflect upon some of the inherent dissimilarities in counseling God's way versus counseling man's way. These include:

- God as the Counselor versus man as the counselor
- Discipleship and sanctification as the purposes of godly counseling versus enhancement of self-esteem or establishment of a comfort zone
- God's absolute truths versus man's

dubious theories

- The Holy Spirit as the teacher and transformer versus the human expert
- Prayer versus positive thinking
- Living together and ministering to one another in the body of Christ versus an appointment in a worldly clinic
- Preparing to counsel by growing spiritually versus advancing intellectually in human wisdom
- Developing a new life in Christ versus attempting to improve the old life in Adam (through self-help and self-hope)
- Thinking with the mind of Christ versus playing human mind games
- Learning to stand in victory over the enemy of men's souls versus trying to use the enemy's theories to live free of his domination
- Having a Wonderful Counselor who created us, died for us, forgave us, and lives in us versus a well-intended, but fallible, human being

Yes, there is an astounding contrast of substance and power between these two counseling perspectives. If we likened the glorious realities of counseling God's way to a heavenly gold mine, the psychological counseling of man would be like an earthly gravel pit. If we likened God's resources to a biblical fountain of living water, man's philosophical wisdom would be like a stagnant pool of contaminated water.

What would the results be in the body of Christ, if we redirected the time, attention, and energies that have been going into these arenas of man-centered help and hope? Instead, what if we invested our all into biblical mining of heavenly gold and spiritual drinking of living water that is found in our Wonderful Counselor and His pure word? We would definitely see **multitudes set free and made whole**. We would no doubt see **a revolution within the Christian counseling ministry**. Ultimately, we would probably see **a broad and deep spiritual reformation throughout the family of God**. The church of Jesus Christ needs it, and the Lord would be greatly glorified through it. **Let us pray for such a reformation** and **make ourselves personally available to God** for His use in accomplishing it!

OTHER MINISTRY RESOURCES
by Pastor Bob Hoekstra
are available from
LIVING IN CHRIST MINISTRIES
P. O. BOX 127, MURRIETA, CA 92564

BOOKS

- The Psychologizing of the Faith

6-TAPE AUDIO BIBLE STUDY ALBUMS

- Counseling God's Way
  *(What Counseling Is - God's Way in
  Counseling - Foundational Truths for
  Counseling God's Way #1 -
  Foundational Truths #2 - Major Threats
  to Counseling God's Way - The
  Counseling Situation)*

- Family God's Way
  *(Two Becoming One - Family Life -
  Worldly Threats to the Family -
  Husbands and Wives - Parents and
  Children - The Lord as Home-Builder)*

- Growing in the Grace of God
  *(The Law of God - The Grace of God -
  Living Daily by the Grace of God - The
  Holy Spirit and the Grace of God -
  Grace for Knowing God - The "Much
  More" Grace of God)*

- God's Sufficiency for Godly Living
  *(Living by God's Sufficiency -
  Characteristics of Living by God's*

Sufficiency - Man's Sufficiency versus God's Sufficiency - Insufficient Vessels Containing Sufficient Treasure - Old Testament Examples of God's Sufficiency - Resurrected Living by God's Sufficiency)

- The Church: How Jesus Builds It
  (Nature, Purpose, and Function of the Church - The Head and the Body - Gifts and Fruit in Ministry - Ministry to the Church - Ministry to the World - Being Equipped for Ministry)

- Contending for the Faith
  (Contending for the Faith - The Exaltation of Self - Misconceptions about Faith - The Health and Wealth Gospel - Psychologizing the Faith - The Unity of the Faith)

- Promise Believers
  (Man's Promises or God's Promises - A God of Promises (Old Testament) - A God of Promises (New Testament) - Unpopular Promises - Children of Promise - Exceedingly Great and Precious Promises)

VIDEO TAPE ALBUMS

- Counseling God's Way
  (What Counseling Is - God's Way in Counseling - Foundational Truths for Counseling God's Way #1 - Foundational Truths #2 - Major Threats

to Counseling God's Way - The
Counseling Situation)

- Growing in the Grace of God
  (The Law of God - The Grace of God -
  Living Daily by the Grace of God - The
  Holy Spirit and the Grace of God -
  Grace for Knowing God - The "Much
  More" Grace of God)

- The Church: How Jesus Builds It
  (Nature, Purpose, and Function of the
  Church - The Head and the Body - Gifts
  and Fruit in Ministry - Ministry to the
  Church - Ministry to the World - Being
  Equipped for Ministry)

- NOTE: Other 6-Tape Bible Study series are
  now in video production.

24-TAPE AUDIO IN-DEPTH BIBLE STUDY ALBUMS

- Counseling God's Way

- Growing in the Grace of God

- Contending for the Faith

OTHER STUDIES

- A variety of 2-Tape and 4-Tape Audio Bible
  Study Albums are also available.

LICM NEWSLETTER

- A free quarterly Newsletter is available by
  contacting Living in Christ Ministries.